THE GREAT BANK ROBBERY

A robust banking ecosystem commensurate to the Indian state's diversities is a perfect recipe for a sustainable economic model. Yet, the question remains: how does the dereliction of duties on the part of auditors and governance custodians affect the financial health of the nation? This book, with elements of humour, communicates such a complex topic in an engaging style and with clarity.

—**Subramanian Swamy,** Former Cabinet Minister, Economist and Author

This book not just describes those Himalayan-scale banking scams of our times but also offers simple explanations of different concepts in the banking parlance while explaining the modus operandi of those scandals. It calls out how poor policymaking and institutional failure are the root causes of growing NPAs in the banking sector. All systems and regulation and supervision mechanisms failed until it reached alarming proportions.

I enjoyed the two-in-one model presentation. More importantly, the writing avoids jargon; simple non-technical terms have been used to describe the ideas and events. I recommend readers pick it up for accessing condensed details concerning bad loans, which are otherwise scattered at many places making it cumbersome to develop a good understanding of such scams.

—**Amar Patnaik**, MP (Rajya Sabha) and Former Principal Accountant General

Adequate finance for promising projects is essential for faster development. There are those who game the banking system by colluding with officials to take loans that they have no intention of repaying. Each write-off of a loan by a bank means much less money for honest and societally beneficial businesses and individuals. The book by two experts is both a post-mortem of past mistakes and misdeeds and a review of what is needed to avoid repeating that dismal history. The book is required reading for those interested in understanding the past and future of banking in India. V. Pattabhi Ram and Sabyasachee Dash merit our praise for their scholarship and presentation of facts.

—**Madhav Das Nalapat**, UNESCO Peace Chair, Manipal University

Probably the book *The Great Bank Robbery: NPAs, Scams and the Future of Regulation* is a follow-up of earlier books, such as *The Scam: Who Won, Who Lost, Who Got Away* and a series of articles in *The Indian Express* by Sucheta Dalal and Debashis Basu on how the corporate sector have looted the commercial and public sector banks.

The book also shows how the regulators have failed to check the extent of the taxpayers' money deposited in the banking system is at risk. The RBI's inspection system has also let down the depositors.

I hope the present book will alert the regulators and investigating agencies of the faltering financial institutions and how they should tighten their internal audit controls. The authors need to be complimented on their effort to focus on the failing controls in the present banking regulations.

—**B.V. Kumar**, Former Member, Central Board of Excise and Customs (CBEC), Special Secretary, Ministry of Finance (MoF) and Former Directorate General (DG), Directorate of Revenue Intelligence (DRI), Narcotics Control Bureau (NCB) and Economic Intelligence Bureau (EIB)

Huge amount of NPAs in Indian banking industry has been a major cause of concern in recent times. Thanks to Asset Quality Review undertaken by the RBI under Dr Raghuram Rajan that real magnitude of problem came to light.

This book is a good-hearted refresher of these scams. It clearly reveals how poor policymaking has been the prime source of nourishment for the NPA virus to grow increasingly virulent. I enjoyed the simple way this book discusses the topics and its innovative format.

—**Amarjit Chopra**, Fellow Chartered Accountant

The Great Bank Robbery explains the nuances and intricacies of banking lucidly, the understanding of which is necessary not just for banking professionals but also for anybody dealing with economic offences. Economic offences and financial crimes have taken centre stage in India's criminal justice system. Documenting and understanding the 11 scams is crucial, 'lest we forget' they took place. I would recommend this to be a must-read for every banker and anybody who deals with financial crimes.

—**Tarun Gulati**, Senior Advocate

A unique attempt that takes the readers through the past, present and the future of the Indian banking system. The authors have used a mix of fiction and current events to address a complex topic in a very creative manner.

—**Aashish Chandorkar**, Public Policy Commentator

THE GREAT BANK ROBBERY

NPAs, SCAMS AND THE FUTURE OF REGULATION

V. PATTABHI RAM AND
SABYASACHEE DASH

RUPA

First published by
Rupa Publications India Pvt. Ltd 2023
7/16, Ansari Road, Daryaganj
New Delhi 110002

Sales Centres:

Allahabad Bengaluru Chennai
Hyderabad Jaipur Kathmandu
Kolkata Mumbai

H-ISBN: 978-93-5702-054-1
E-ISBN: 978-93-5702-059-6

First impression 2023

10 9 8 7 6 5 4 3 2 1

The moral right of the authors has been asserted.

Printed in India

Dedicated to
Sadgurudev, Swami Shree Sadananda Saraswati

CONTENTS

Foreword   *ix*
Preface   *xiii*
Prologue   *xvii*

Part One
Setting the Trap

1. The Stephens Chat   3
2. Moon, Money and Madam   11
3. Banks and Barbers   17
4. Multiple Balance Sheet Problems   30
5. How Banks Make Profits: Part 1   36
6. How Banks Make Profits: Part 2   44
7. Krishna Revises His Notes   55

Part Two
Scamming the Bank

8. Mundhra and Nagarwala: Conmen   59
9. Harshad Mehta: The Pied Piper   66
10. Ketan Parekh: The Bombay Bull   78
11. Vijay Mallya: Grounded   86
12. Anil Ambani: From Hero to Zero   95
13. IL&FS: Infrastructure Runs into a Roadblock   102
14. Nirav Modi: Diamonds Aren't Forever   111
15. DHFL: Mortgage Major's Muddle   120
16. No to Yes Bank   127
17. PMC Bank: Uncooperative Banks   133
18. Lakshmi Vilas Bank: The House of Wealth   142
19. Krishna Begins His Draft   150

Part Three
Sleeping at the Wheel?

20. Where Were the Auditors?   155
21. How Independent Are Independent Directors?   165
22. Who Will Rate the Raters?   174
23. RBI: The God That Slipped   183
24. Krishna Returns to His Notes   191
25. Getting Bulletproof   194

Acknowledgements   201
Index   203

FOREWORD

In the 1969 western film *The Great Bank Robbery*, robbers seek to steal gold from a bank's vault in Texas. A preacher is the thief. The robbery is scheduled to take place during the 4th of July celebrations. Evidence of a banker's corruption is also hidden in the vault and a lady protagonist rides nude (like Lady Godiva) to cause distraction.

V. Pattabhi Ram and Sabyasachee Dash may not have intended an allusion to the film, but this book, on non-performing assets (NPAs), scams and the future of regulation, has parallels with that film. For a start, there have been a handful of books on banks, scams and NPAs, but none of them begins in such a striking and fictionalized way. The first chapter, 'The Stephens Chat', set in the future of 2036, grips the reader's attention and, in Part I, we are led through a very novel way of explaining the history of banking and the cooking of books. Those who preach are often thieves and corruption by bankers is hidden away in vaults not open to the public eye. Can the financial sector's growth (the financial sector has non-banks too) be disproportionately high, compared to that of the real sector? Or must there be some balance between the two? Incrementally, banking was liberalized in the 1990s, with new private sector commercial banks.

However, particularly in the 2000s, regulatory norms were relaxed and banks (particularly public sector ones) became lax about credit appraisal and due diligence. Like the 4th of July celebrations, the economy was roaring, raring to go. This was the deflection and misdirection magicians are wont to do, breaking down the link between real and financial sectors. The cycle turned. Fall in commodity prices affected sectors like steel.

Public–private partnerships in infrastructure meant over-leveraged firms defaulted when things turned sour. The asset quality of banks deteriorated and NPAs mounted. The numbers reveal the story, manifest since 2015, with stressed assets (a broader definition than NPAs) assuming horrendous proportions. In hindsight and ex-post, we know what should have been discerned ex-ante. Ex-post, misgovernance has been laid bare, like the lady protagonist in the film stripping.

Look Back in Anger was a 1959 film, though the successful play preceded it, in 1956. Most citizens have little to do with scams, directly. The Insolvency and Bankruptcy Code (IBC) was enacted in 2016, forcing errant promoters to exit, for the first time ever. Reforms are about competition, requiring both entry and exit. Exit hurts, through haircuts, with citizens indirectly (there are some direct examples too) suffering, because any cost borne by public sector banks is borne by the public exchequer. The same argument holds for bailouts and recapitalization. In the 1956/59 play/film, the protagonist watches helplessly as reality bites. There is no further resemblance, beyond the title.

One thinks of films because that's the way the book is written, like a script. Throughout Part I, situated in 2036, we look back in anger, as the authors reveal the nuts and bolts of how everything raveled and unraveled.

Anatomy of a Scandal isn't a film, but a 2008 novel, adapted into a TV series that is a thriller. Indirectly affected by scams and scandals, a citizen has a vicarious interest when such incidents are reported in the media and there is helpless fulmination and rage at such scamsters having seemingly got away scot-free. Expanding on the skeletal nuts and bolts of Part I, Part II adds the flesh and blood, the anatomy of 11 scams. There is a long history of scams in independent India. Understandably, these focus on banks and the financial sector. The human mind is prone to myopia. We remember the immediate, while the past slips into distant memory. In a deviation from this principle, one of the 11 scams discussed is about Mundhra and Nagarwala, described as conmen. Mundhra clearly belongs. As the first financial scam in independent India, the case established the nexus between business and bureaucracy. The Nagarwala fraud was different in nature. The other 10 are of recent vintage—scams we will immediately recall. With reforms and financial sector liberalization, scams have increased in number, as well as in nominal values. The mind boggles at the figures. Is this an argument against liberalization? It cannot be. Instead, the argument is about regulatory failure. Written in the style of a thriller, the book teaches how frauds took place and about regulatory loopholes that could be exploited. It doesn't delve much into the legal system, which is also part of the jigsaw.

In post-mortems, we know about regulatory failure at the Reserve Bank of India (RBI). But the rest of it is about corporate misgovernance at the level of boards, independent directors, auditors and rating agencies. This is documented in Part III. There is of course the clichéd quote from *The Adventure of Silver Blaze*, with a conversation between Sherlock Holmes and Inspector Gregory of Scotland Yard.

> Gregory: Is there any other point to which you would wish to draw my attention?
> Holmes: To the curious incident of the dog in the night-time.
> Gregory: The dog did nothing in the night-time.
> Holmes: That was the curious incident.

The authors tell us about the dogs that should have barked, but did not. Clearly, this means we need a different kind of dog, or a dog with a different kind of training. Post-mortems are easy, with the benefit of 20/20 vision, in hindsight. The purpose of regulation and law is to act as a deterrent, to prevent *mala fide* action in the future. This valuable book will help shape informed debate to that end. Before plugging loopholes, one has to know what they are, though there is also the generic point that crooks are always one step ahead of regulation and law. If one loophole is plugged, another will be found. There exist books on specific scams. Harshad Mehta being a case in point. But I can't readily think of books that straddle a variety of scams. On that count alone, V. Pattabhi Ram and Sabyasachee Dash have produced a remarkable book, so that citizen angst and government countervailing action is better informed.

Bibek Debroy
Economist and Chairman of the Economic
Advisory Council to the Prime Minister of India
12 December 2022

PREFACE

One of the best experiences during 2020–21, amidst the *tandav* of Covid-19, remains writing this book. As chartered accountants (CAs), it was natural we picked the subject of money, and given the seismic shift in the banking ecosystem, and our belief that this space will see a tsunami of actions, we chose *The Great Bank Robbery*.

While writing this book, one of the guiding principles has been to state concepts and facts in a non-technical manner, so that even readers unfamiliar with the nuances of banking find it interesting. Towards this, we have relied on public information. Significant insights have been imported from conversations with experienced auditors, bankers, taxmen, authors, and others.

Fraud is a fascinating subject as long as you are not the victim, and if it is communicated with the right mix of facts and gossip, it can be quite exciting. We have tried to keep things engaging while steering clear of market masala. We believe who we vote for has nothing to do with what has happened in the banking world, and the objective is to stay with facts.

This book explores the setting in which a bank works, the scandals that rocked the banking world, and the role of special players, such as auditors, bankers, credit rating agencies and directors. It then walks through a probable future. In short, it is about context, culprits, *chowkidar*s and crystal ball gazing. The concepts are packaged in a quasi-formal conversation mode to keep the readability intact: a family with people from different generations indulges in discussions over several sessions during a winter holiday.

Part I, namely 'Setting the Trap', explains how banks operate. It describes ideas such as statutory liquidity ratio (SLR), cash reserve ratio (CRR), capital to risk weighted assets ratio (CRAR), spread, etc., and how these determine liquidity, solvency and profitability. It also suggests how in this scheme of things, the rise of bad loans is inevitable.

Part II, namely 'Scamming the Bank', summarizes 11 notorious frauds that stunned banks. These show that the more things change, the more they remain the same.

Part III focusses on the role of special players or chowkidars. They are the auditors, bankers, credit raters and directors. Can these men escape moral responsibility even if the needle of culpability does not turn decisively towards them? We then close out with crystal ball gazing. What are the banking world's gathering storms? What will banks look like in the future?

India has contributed to banking in a big way. Its gift of the number zero to humanity was, in a way, the starting point. The Roman numerals were complicated, which made account keeping and consequently banking very complicated. The introduction of the Hindu-Arabic numerals made life simpler and also allowed the use of decimals. The metric system helped calculate interest— the core of banking—far more efficiently and encouraged the proliferation of moneylending and banks. Let's recall what Albert Einstein said, 'We owe a lot to the Indians, who taught us how to count, without which no worthwhile scientific discovery could have been made.'[1]

The world has moved a considerable distance in the last 17 years. In 2006, the global gross domestic product (GDP) was $51.78 trillion. Since then, it has snowballed and by 2021 amounted to $96.1 trillion,[2] and the market capitalization estimated at $93.69 trillion.[3] By 2021, the global GDP touched $91.1 trillion, and is

---

[1]'Some Famous Quotes That Perfectly Define the Idea of India', News18, 14 August 2016, https://bit.ly/3Uyywlb. Accessed on 16 November 2022.
[2]'GDP (current US$)', The World Bank, https://bit.ly/3s7GRzR. Accessed on 20 October 2022.
[3]'Market Capitalization of Listed Domestic Companies (Current US$)', The World

just a striking distance from the magic figure of $100 trillion. The International Monetary Fund places the number at an estimated $104 for calendar year 2022.[4]

However, this is just the tip of the iceberg. With automation, artificial intelligence, machine learning, blockchain, cloud computing, cognitive technology, digitalization, etc., becoming realities, the next few years will be the most exciting period in history. Just as a certain generation hardly stepped into a bank to draw money, generations in the future might never see a bank at all, relying instead on online resources.

We believe that when you finish reading *The Great Bank Robbery,* you will have a sense of what had actually gone wrong and what precautions we must take, or rather should have taken, to keep things right.

Happy reading.

Bank, https://bit.ly/3CHALee. Accessed on 20 October 2022.
[4]Koop, Avery, 'The $100 Trillion Global Economy in One Chart', Visual Capitalist, 12 July 2022, https://bit.ly/3Ihd1C5. Accessed on 2 January 2023.

PROLOGUE

24 December 2036.

In Dalal Street, the seat of India's equity market, the stock price of the National Bank of Hindustan (NBH) price has crashed. Until yesterday, the scrip was famously called the 'banker's bank' for its sheer safety. Today, the forensic auditors' report leaked, causing mayhem in the market. The share price dropped into a bottomless pit, with more quantity coming up on the selling block without a corresponding number of buys.

History was repeating itself. The NBH was India's second-largest bank. It held an unprecedented quantum of non-performing assets (NPAs), partly due to bad business judgement and mainly on account of frauds and creative accounting practices.

Law enforcers forced their way into the home of two of the partners who had signed the bank's financial statements in the capacity of statutory auditors and took them into custody. In recent years, these auditors gave clean reports on the NBH. Such reports suggested fair and transparent financials complying with generally accepted accounting principles (GAAP).

A hurriedly convened council meeting of the Institute of Chartered Accountants of India (ICAI) took stock of the developing story and made known its initial disappointment.

The rating agencies had marked every instrument issued by the bank at the AAA (Triple-A) level for 'highest safety', which is the highest possible rating that an instrument can have. Such rating is given to those instruments that carry the maximum levels of creditworthiness. It was on the market grapevine that their managing directors would be called in for questioning. Journalists suddenly talked about imaginary assets being present and actual liabilities absent in the balance sheet.

The independent directors were marquee names. Three of them—a strategy professor, a corporate czar and a media baron— left the board on a nudge from the government.

India was agog with rumours that Angelina Das, the finance minister, would step down, owning moral responsibility. 'It will shield the prime minister,' remarked a noisy opinion-maker in a charged debate during prime time on national television.

Saloni Mehta, the curly-haired Reserve Bank of India (RBI) governor, was at the Prime Minister's Office (PMO). She was a beloved public figure, appreciated for her professional competence and wit. Speculation was rife that she would resign. No such thing happened.

As the maelstrom gained momentum and threatened to engulf the economy, the Stephens, India's foremost banking family, sat down to discuss the issue.

PART ONE

SETTING THE TRAP

1

THE STEPHENS CHAT

25 December 2036
Panjim, Goa

Eighty-nine-year-old Lobin Stephen Senior cozied up in his reclining chair, reading the latest copy of the *Business Standard*, a cup of piping hot coffee in his hand. Horn-rimmed spectacles sat atop the bridge of his nose. He didn't look his age. Physically fit to give even 50-year-olds a run for their points in a game of squash, Senior had just returned from his mandatory morning walk. The pink paper[1] carried the banking scandal that had broken out at the country's top bank. As he sipped on the caffeine, he recalled the many scandals he had seen, read about and discussed over the last 70 years.

The Stephens were a family of bankers. While the patriarch was the former chairman of a leading global bank, his daughter, Larissa Iqbal, now 65, was the former chief executive officer (CEO) of a top private bank. Laura Merchant, 41, the sole third-generation woman, headed a billion-dollar microfinance company. Her son, Lobin Stephen Junior, born in 2017, two years before Covid-19 struck the world, was currently a Harvard student who planned on interning at JPMorgan Chase. Junior's second cousin, Krishna McKenzie, now a 13-year-old, loved the game of Monopoly, especially playing the banker.

Today, for Christmas, they had all assembled at the family

---

[1]A term used to denote business papers. In 1893, the *Financial Times* first began printing on pink paper to distinguish it from its main rival, the *Financial News*.

home. Seated on the floor in front of Senior was the youngest of the bunch, Krishna, itching to hear stories from him. He was always bubbling with energy and full of questions. Giving him company was Junior, who, too, had parked himself on the floor, eagerly waiting to listen to the Grand Old Banker.

'GGP,' (short for 'great-grandpa') said Junior. 'The opinion makers on YouTube are screaming that the NBH is the mother of all banking frauds and is the first of its kind. Is that right? I saw an acerbic panel discussion where they even accused someone in our family of being involved.'

'Well, not exactly,' said the elder banker, looking up from his paper. 'Scandals and bank failures have always been a part of life. With time, they only grow bigger and scarier. It is not as though only banks of today default. History is full of such stories. And the culprits are almost always the same.'

'Tell me one, tell me one,' said the youngest, the one they lovingly called 'Brat'. Excitement twinkled in his eyes—he loved these stories.

Senior took another sip of the coffee, set aside the newspaper and switched to storytelling mode. 'The earliest one I read about was from my school days, which dates back to the time of the Sepoy Mutiny, in 1857. You must have heard of that. It is also regarded as India's First War of Independence.'

'You were once young enough to go to school?' There was a childlike innocence in Krishna's question.

Junior placed a finger on his lips and said, 'Shush! Don't interrupt.'

Senior continued, 'Those were the times when many cotton companies sprung up in Bombay.'

'Where is Bombay?'

'Mumbai was once called Bombay. It is the financial capital of India and was renamed in 1995 to reflect the name of Mumba Devi, the Hindu goddess.'

Krishna scribbled it down on the notepad that he always

carried with him. He had an insatiable thirst for information.

'The rise and rise of cotton companies led to a steep demand for capital or money. A company can raise money in three forms: equity capital, preference capital and debt capital. Equity capital is brought in by equity shareholders. Preference shareholders bring in preference capital. Lenders such as banks, financial institutions and individuals provide loans to a company, and these are called debt capital. Together, equity, preference and debt constitute a company's capital.

'What happened next?' asked Krishna.

'The Bank of Bombay, established in 1840 in the Bombay Presidency, began to lend recklessly. It lent against shares, and at times even against personal security.

'A bank usually takes over a business's properties as security. This gives the bank a right to sell those properties, if the business defaults on its loan. Shares of a company can be placed as collateral to raise loans. This is however risky because share prices fluctuate every day. Banks also lend against personal security, which refers to the borrower or a third party's guarantee. A loan against personal guarantee is risky. Bankers should desist from it unless the borrower has a long relationship with the bank.

'All of a sudden, as demand for cotton dropped, production slowed down, profits fell and cashflows began to evaporate. Little wonder, the banks went bust.'

'Just like that?' asked Junior.

'Yes, just like that.'

'What is the lesson from this?'

'Simple. Do not overextend balance sheets. It means do not overborrow or over lend. Assets and liabilities are elastic only up to a point. Remember, if you stretch an elastic band too far, it will snap. Similarly, stretch a bank with bad loans and accounting frauds, and it is bound to go kaput.'

'GGP, where were you when this happened?' It was Krishna.

'This was much before I was born. I came to this world only

in 1947, and this happened almost 90 years before that, in the 1860s.'

The little one winked at his cousin. For him, GGP was both ancient and immortal. He scribbled something in his notepad, and said, 'I guess bankers learnt their lesson.'

'Well, far from it, dear, far from it. History is a great teacher, but people often fail to learn from it,' sighed Junior even as Krishna stared at him, unbelieving and disapproving of his interjections.

'I am a tad tired and want to catch forty winks. I made a short note on this topic years ago, based on newspaper write-ups and personal jottings. It's on the reading table of my study room. Read it. We will meet at noon.' He then stood up and walked down to this bedroom.

In his notepad, Krishna wrote, '**LESSON:** Do not ever overextend balance sheets.' Junior peeped into it and laughed.

'What about the charge that the Stephens are involved?' shouted Krishna suddenly. 'That makes no sense. No Stephen has ever worked with the NHB.'

'These days, these anchors come up with anything,' said Senior, pausing. 'Once upon a time, your mother was the deputy CEO of the bank. That is the closest connection the Stephens had with India's mega bank.'

Of course, that wasn't the whole truth. Like King Yudhishthira in the Mahabharata told Guru Drona that Ashwatthama was dead without mentioning that he was referring to an elephant and not to his son, GGP only revealed what was essential while concealing the vital.

———◈◈◈———

THE CRISIS AIN'T NEW... AND SOME HISTORY

Which is the world's oldest bank? That depends on how you define 'bank'—it could either be when the institution originated or when it was designated as a bank.

If it is the former, then Banca Monte dei Paschi di Siena wins hands down. For over 150 years, since 1472, it was an institutional pawnbroker, which raised money from charity and lent it to the needy against collaterals. In 1624, Banca changed to its present form as a bank.

Berenberg Bank is the oldest institution to be officially designated as a bank. Founded in 1590, it has operated continuously with the same family. Banca is now a retail bank, while Berenberg is an investment bank.

The Medicis of Italy were the first family to undertake banking. The Medici Bank, established in 1397, flourished for over a hundred years, emerging as the biggest and most respected bank in Europe. It popularized double-entry bookkeeping, invented the letter of credit and pioneered the idea of a holding company—three great modern themes, and the Medicis had a role in it.

In the mid-1860s, the British turned to the Indian cotton markets as the US civil war affected imports. New companies and banks sprung up in Calcutta. Banks lent recklessly, including to private companies and against personal guarantee. They adopted creative accounting, which involves using practices that bend the law without breaking it, to hide their recklessness. They use the loopholes to portray a better financial health of the company than the reality. Some quick examples include recognizing revenue ahead of time, delaying the recording of expenses, masking contingent liability and not making adequate provision for doubtful debts. Lately, this tool has been used to camouflage goof-ups without being overtly violative of broad governing regulations and accounting practices.

Coming back to the story of the Calcutta banks, when the client's business inevitably failed, many blamed it on the fact that banks had 'unlimited liability'. That was funny, because unlimited liability should have made the bankers ever more cautious because on a collapse, the owners would have to make good the shortage from their private funds.

In 1861, the British, who then ruled India, allowed banks to have limited liability. If you thought it was the perfect medication, you were wrong. Banks continued to fall by the wayside across the board, unconnected with ownership, as both private and public sector banks failed in equal measure. The Bank of Bombay is a case in point. It showed that regulations can help banks be prudent in their activity only to a limited extent. You need to have a suitable gene to not take undue risks.

Incidentally, here is a quick distinction between limited and unlimited liability. The former includes a limit on the liability of the members better known as shareholders. Their liability is restricted to the sum they paid for their shares or the amount of the guarantee. In the case of the latter, there is no limit on the liability of members. In other words, they will be called upon to pay from their personal wealth as well.

In 1905, the Swadeshi Movement called on desi banks to fund desi enterprises. The response was overwhelming, as banks sprung up. By 1913, there were 451[2] of them.

However, soon a few banks, such as the Indian Specie Bank, collapsed. Analysts said that had the banks' management released the balance sheets on time, the fraud could have been detected early! Sounds like a deja vu?

The next 54 years—coinciding with the onset of the First World War (1914) and culminating with the Green Revolution in India (1968)—saw the failure of about 1,800 banks.[3] The principal culprits were from Kerala, West Bengal and the Madras Presidency (particularly Tamil Nadu, Andhra Pradesh and Telangana). Somewhere along the line, people felt that if India had a central bank, the collapses would stop.

In 1935, that prayer was answered with the establishment of the

[2]Agrawal, Amol, 'Banking Crises: An Indian History', *Mint*, 26 February 2018, https://bit.ly/3TzFfdz. Accessed on 20 October 2022.
[3]Ibid.

Reserve Bank of India (RBI) through the Reserve Bank of India Act, 1934. By then (between 1913 and 1934), 350 banks had closed shop across the country. The RBI could not stem the tide, and in the next 12 years, 900 banks failed. The mess continued as 665 more banks fell by the wayside between the period of Indian independence in 1947 and nationalization in 1969.

Meanwhile, in 1949, the Banking Regulation Act was enacted, which provided the central bank with some teeth. Statutory liquidity ratio (SLR) was introduced as a tool to create reserve capital. SLR is the minimum percentage of deposits that a commercial bank has to maintain in the form of liquid cash, gold or other securities. This percentage is mandatory and is set by the RBI. It is one of the statutory weapons available in the RBI's armoury to regulate liquidity in the economy. All banks, both old and new, now had to apply to the RBI for a licence. Unfortunately, in 1960, when Palai Central Bank, a commercial bank headquartered in Kerala, went belly-up, the regulator panicked and enforced significant closures.

In 1951, there were 566 banks, of which 474 were declared unfit to be in the RBI's Second Schedule: these banks were running their business detrimental to the interests of depositors and the RBI had to come down on them.[4]

In 1967, the number dropped to 91 banks. Two years later came nationalization, which arguably sowed a rotten seed in the banking system. Several good things can be attributed to nationalization, although Indira Gandhi's critics accused her of making an economic virtue out of political necessity to consolidate her political capital.

Post-nationalization, no new licence was issued till 1994. During this phase, the government aggressively pushed bankers to take the early steps towards 'financial inclusion'. Alas, this step translated into loan melas, which eventually led to bad loans.

In 1994, when India was in the middle of the first generation of

---

[4]Gupta, Shatakshi, 'Banking Failures in India', TrendingNews, 11 March 2020, https://bit.ly/3Fs7A0i. Accessed on 12 November 2022.

reforms, 10 new banks were licenced, thus marking the arrival of private sector banks. The event would change the face of Indian banking forever. In the early 2000s, two more banks received the nod, and in 2014, another two got added to the list.

Bank failures continued. A slew of cooperative banks bit the dust, and a few public sector and other banks almost pulled down shutters. In many cases, the government came in as the white knight in shining armour. Weak banks were merged with strong ones. There were collapses, acquisitions, mergers and consolidations, which indicated that not everything was hunky-dory with the banking system.

The RBI had a slew of strong, articulate and well-meaning governors, because of whom India fended off the global financial crisis and managed to hold the banking sector from falling in the years following that.

2

MOON, MONEY AND MADAM

At around 11.30 in the morning, Krishna asked Junior to wake up his GGP, so that they could hear more stories of bank failures. However, Junior was unwilling to disturb the 89-year-old former banker's nap.

Slightly irritated, Krishna decided to take matter into his hands. He knocked at Senior's door and was pleasantly surprised to see him dressed and ready to pick up the conversation from where they had left it.

'I told you, no? GGP is known for his punctuality and determination to keep his word,' said Junior.

Krishna blinked. 'But when did you say that?'

'Well, when you were hogging that ice-cream like a greedy pig.'

Krishna wasn't amused and promised himself that someday, not too far away, he would have his revenge on his cousin.

◆

They all gathered in Lobin Stephen Senior's study, from where the man did his day's work of mentoring young bankers, writing the odd article and getting ready to deliver talks over video-conferencing to a global audience.

'So, where were we?' asked Senior.

'You had left the story somewhere in the nineteenth century and asked us to read your handwritten materials, which we did,' answered Krishna.

'Well, 1969 is an important year, as it marked a watershed moment in our nation's history.'

'What happened that year?' Krishna asked, scratching his head.

'It marks the hundredth birth anniversary of Mahatma Gandhi, Brat,' remarked Junior.

'It was also a watershed year in world history,' added Senior.

Junior got into the groove. 'On 20 July 1969, American astronauts Neil Armstrong and Edwin Aldrin became the first men to walk on the moon. Along with Michael Collins, they were propelled into space and history—'

'Come on, what has that got to do with banks?' interrupted Krishna. 'Why are you getting into this whole elocution mode?'

Senior smiled. 'Possibly nothing, or possibly something.'

'Are you by any chance referring to bank nationalization?' asked Junior.

'Yes, you are absolutely right. Have you heard of Indira Gandhi?' he turned his attention to Krishna.

'Yes, India's first and the world's second woman prime minister after Sirima Ratwatte Dias Bandaranaike, commonly known as Sirimavo Bandaranaike, of Sri Lanka.'

'The day before Armstrong landed on the moon, Mrs Gandhi had made an announcement that would change the future of banking.

'On 19 July 1969, at 8.30 p.m. IST, she addressed the nation on radio and announced the nationalization of banks. The acting president, V.V. Giri, who was serving his last day in office, signed the ordinance, bringing 14 banks under government ownership, and accounting for 85 per cent of the total resources of the system. This was socialism at its very best, or at its very worst, depending upon where your political ideologies lay. By the way, I.G. Patel, who would later become an RBI governor, wrote Mrs Gandhi's speech, to its last comma.'

After gulping down a glass of chilled water, Senior resumed his storytelling.

'Mrs Gandhi wasn't done with her brand of socialism yet. During the Indo-Pak War of 1971, the foreign-owned oil companies refused to supply fuel to both the Indian Army and Indian Air Force. The Iron Lady of India, as Mrs Gandhi was called, responded by nationalizing the oil companies. Oil majors, such as the Indian Oil Corporation, Hindustan Petroleum Corporation Ltd and Bharat Petroleum Corporation, were now required to keep a minimum stock level of oil to be supplied to the military when needed.

'Eleven years later, in 1980, in her third term in office, she added six more banks that took the tally to 20. Meanwhile, when she was reelected in 1971, she spread her net farther, nationalizing the insurance sector.'

Krishna turned to face his cousin. 'You are studying at Harvard. Do you not know about these?'

Junior smiled. 'Well, I read about this in my Class XII economics. And my view is that the first bank nationalization set in motion a chain of events, which possibly triggered the sticky situation that we got into in the mid-2010s. Mrs Gandhi's critics called nationalization the "original sin"[5] and said it kicked off lemon socialism.'

'Lemon socialism? Are you taking me for a ride?' Krishna asked, a little suspicious of his cousin's intentions.

Senior was in splits at the little one's anger. 'Lemon socialism is a contemptuous term for a form of government intervention in which it subsidizes failing firms, and the taxpayer absorbs the losses. In other words, profits are privatized and losses are socialized.'

Junior continued from where he had left. 'In a way, I think Madam Gandhi was right. Had we bought into Adam Smith's concept of market economy, we may not have seen the geographical spread of the banks to the eight corners of India: north, east, west, south, northeast, southeast, southwest and northwest—'

---

[5]'Bank Nationalisation: The Original Sin?' *BQ Prime*, 19 July 2019, https://bit.ly/3Bsn8jr. Accessed on 12 November 2022.

'Who is Adam Smith?' Krishna interjected.

'What do you study in school? Do you not know that Smith is the father of modern economics? In 1759, he wrote a classic, *The Theory of Moral Sentiments*. In 1776, he backed it with an extremely readable book titled *An Inquiry into the Nature and Causes of the Wealth of Nations.*' Krishna quickly scribbled down the names. 'This summer, read one of them; and in winter read the other.'

'Will I be able to understand?'

'Even you will understand it,' said Junior.

Krishna ignored the jibe. 'So, GGP, was the drive towards nationalization good? Or was it bad?'

'It's time for me to have lunch. I have just forwarded you an article that I wrote on this topic many years ago. Read it, and we will catch up post-lunch,' said Senior, walking towards the dining table. The clock had struck 12.30 in the afternoon. He believed in doing everything on time.

Krishna scribbled in his notepad. **LESSON**: In 1969, Mahatma Gandhi's centenary birthday was celebrated, a man walked on the moon and Mrs Gandhi announced the first wave of bank nationalization.

WAS NATIONALIZATION GOOD ECONOMICS OR GOOD POLITICS?

History records that nationalization increased the number of branches, enhanced the geographical reach of the banking system, increased household savings, brought investment in the informal sector and contributed to regional development. It opened the doors to inclusive banking, took it to unbanked rural areas and helped both the Green Revolution and poverty alleviation. Priority sector lending (PSL) became the new normal. The goal was to provide credit to the less-privileged sections of society, instead of financing only the profitable sectors. Agriculture loans, credit to micro, small and medium enterprises (MSMEs), and housing finance are a few examples of PSL.

However, over the next 50 years, public sector banks incurred heavy losses, showed very obvious signs of inefficiency and worked at the behest of their political masters. In a very strange but definitive way, they laid the seeds of the banking crises relating to bad assets that troubled India and arguably opened up the floodgates of corruption.

All said and done, the larger question remained: should governments be in the business of running businesses instead of focussing on the business of governance?

Let's have a bit of history.

Many believed that Mrs Gandhi's decision to nationalize was a political one and that people favoured it. She saw it as an opportunity to emerge as a stronger leader.

The generation born in the 1990s may not know that in 1966, she got in as a compromise candidate for the country's top political job. Three years later, in 1969, her party, the Congress, had, against her wishes, named N. Sanjiva Reddy as the presidential candidate, which she felt eroded her authority. She wanted to strike back.

Critics call nationalization the 'original sin' and claim it paved the way for wide-scale practice of lemon socialism, i.e., privatizing profits and socializing losses. It raised the mercury level in the debate of good politics versus bad economics. Morarji Desai, the then finance minister, resigned in July 1969 in protest against the nationalization of major banks. Ironically, kingmaker K. Kamaraj, who had prevented Desai from becoming prime minister, so that Mrs Gandhi could hold the top office on Lal Bahadur Shastri's demise, sided with him. In fact, Kamaraj called it '[a] sell-out to Americans'.[6]

Jayaprakash Narayan, best known as JP, who later, in 1974, led the call for Total Revolution against the Prime Minister, praised

[6]Agrawal, Amol, 'Why Indira Gandhi Nationalised India's Banks', *BQ Prime*, 19 July 2019, https://bit.ly/3Fo1w93. Accessed on 12 November 2022.

Mrs Gandhi's judgement on bank nationalization. One of our country's distinguished economists, RBI governor L.K. Jha, too favoured it. The broad consensus was that while economics dictated India to nationalize its banks, the timing of the move was intended to milk it politically.

It should be noted that in those days (pre-1969), businessmen owned banks and lent to themselves, ignoring the masses. Agriculture was too high-risk a sector to lend in. The priority sector was not really a priority. Neither the public nor the government liked this attitude. There was widespread resentment against class banking, which had left the teeming majority unbanked. The call was for mass banking, and Mrs Gandhi, with her grooming in socialism, struck.

Most banks had remained privately owned despite the RBI's control. Businessmen who owned the banks often diverted deposits to their own businesses while omitting the priority sector. In addition, class banking, which excluded the poor (the majority population), was the target of intense hatred in India. Mrs Gandhi stated her desire to nationalize banks in a document titled 'Stray Thoughts on Bank Nationalization'. The paper received big support from the public.

In economic terms, nationalization was a dark cloud with a few silver linings. Some critics believed that public sector banks had become a passport to losses, inefficiency and reckless lending based on phone calls from political masters. It sowed the seeds of corruption. However, in political terms, it was a smashing hit, demolishing the Swatantra Party—which was founded by C. Rajagopalachari, the first and last governor general of independent India, in response to the Congress's increasingly socialist outlook—so comprehensively that few remember it was once a contender to rule India.

3

BANKS AND BARBERS

The trio was bank from lunch.

'The biggest problem with the banking system is the prevalence of non-performing assets, or NPAs,' said Junior. 'Why has this come to such a pass?'

'What is an NPA?' asked Krishna.

'This is why we should not let kids in on our conversation,' said a visibly annoyed Junior.

Senior smiled at Krishna. 'How much money do you have with you?'

'₹15,000, GGP. I made that money running a few errands for the elders in the family.'

'Will you give ₹10,000 from it to your cousin, Junior?'

Krishna looked in the direction of Junior. 'Yes, if he repays ₹1,000 per month over the next 12 months.'

'What if he pays for three months and does not pay on the fourth?'

'I will follow up with him, GGP.'

'What if he does not pay on the fourth or the fifth?'

'I will threaten to tell his friends that he borrowed from me, and isn't repaying.'

'What if he doesn't pay on the sixth month?'

'I will complain to his mother.'

'What if he continues to default in the seventh month?'

'I think I will deliver a stinging slap.'

Junior couldn't help laughing at the reference to a stinging slap. 'Well, in corporate life, you cannot act like a thug. There is something called the National Company Law Tribunal, or NCLT. I am sure GGP will tell you about that.'

Krishna felt relieved. For a moment, he had thought he had crossed the line by referring to a slap.

Senior picked up the thread. 'Well, when you lend money and the borrower either stops paying interest or repaying the principal, it's a warning that your investment may turn sour. In banking language, such a loan is called an NPA.

'Any loan that ceases to give a return for a specified period is an NPA. Generally, that specified time is 90 days, but it may vary with countries, instruments and conditions. Our banking industry is seriously afflicted by the massive amounts of NPAs.'

'So, Junior would be an NPA from the seventh month, GGP?'

'Bang on!'

Krishna looked up from his notes and said, 'Suppose, I lend a friend ₹100,000. He promises to pay ₹9,000 every month the following year. He may honour his commitment, which is good, or he may dishonour it. If the installment is overdue by 90 days, my loan is deemed to have become an NPA.

'It is not that it has gone bad in the sense that my friend will not pay. It is just that as a prudent measure, I will regard that as a warning sign of impending default. And based on a pre-determined formula, I will decide how much interest income should be taken to the profit and loss accounts,' said Krishna.

The last sentence was a shot in the dark. There was a momentary silence as Krishna looked around for approbation or laughter, depending on how well he had placed things on the table. He was right. Under law, the interest amount to be taken as income in the case of an NPA is based on a pre-laid per cent.

Junior cheered. 'Wisdom from the mouth of babies!'

Krishna grinned and pulled up the collar of his T-shirt in pride.

Senior asked, 'If your cousin didn't pay up an installment on the due date, what could be the reason for it?'

'Maybe he had a genuine difficulty. Or maybe he thought I earned a lot and so wilfully defaulted.'

Junior couldn't help smiling at the reference to wilful default and said, 'Anyway, it is a breach of trust and is likely' to dampen the relationship between the two of us.'

'When this gets extrapolated to loans given by banks,' continued Senior, 'the problem becomes severe. And by the way, there is a small add-on. Normally, the interest amount is taken as income when it becomes receivable, and not necessarily when it is received. Thus for instance, if the interest is receivable on 30 June but is actually received only on 30 August, it will be considered as income in June and not in August.

'So, when a loan becomes an NPA, past interest not received but considered as income will also have to be reversed in the bank's books.'

Junior turned to Krishna. 'Brat, just in case you missed the point: if my borrowing from you becomes an NPA, you will have to write off the loan over the years. Trust you got that?'

'What? Impossible. That's not fair,' said a bewildered Krishna.

'Ha. Ha. That's the law,' said Junior with a flourish.

Krishna was perturbed. He turned to his great-grandfather and said, 'Can I not move the NCLT or whatever it was Junior said?'

Senior smiled. 'No. The NCLT is for moving against companies, and not against individuals. So, if you have lent to a company and it is refusing payment, you can knock on the doors of NCLT. All proceedings under the Companies Act of 2013, such as arbitration, arrangements, compromise, reconstruction and winding up, have to be put up before the NCLT. In short, it is the adjudicating authority for insolvency resolution under the Insolvency and Bankruptcy Code, or IBC.'

'Hmm...' said Krishna, reflectively.

'Well, are the "rules of provisioning" written in stone?' asked Junior. 'Is it possible to change the goalposts and say that under certain circumstances, the 90-day rule will not apply?' He turned towards Krishna and explained, 'Brat, before you ask, provisioning is the process of debiting a part amount of the asset or loan to the profit and loss account.'

Ignoring the explanation, Krishna said, 'No rule is written in stone. Remember, India's constitution has been amended 105 times between 1950 and 2022.'

Senior intervened. 'During Covid-19, the RBI instructed banks not to treat any loan as an NPA. It meant that the asset classification, income recognition and provisioning norms were given a go-by. This instruction came as manna from heaven for the banks, particularly the public sector banks. After all, if the loans are not treated as NPAs, the banks can recognize the interest earned as income. Also, they will not have to provide for bad assets.'

'Well, GGP, is it true that the borrowers moved the Supreme Court demanding that they should not even be charged interest during the pandemic?' Junior sounded incredulous.

'Both yes and no. Yes, because the borrowers wanted a waiver of interest on interest. No, because they were ready to pay regular interest.'

'You mean they were okay with simple interest and not compound interest,' chimed in Krishna.

'Yes, the courts agreed with the borrowers,' said Senior.

'That's so stupid of them.'

'Oh, really? You know better than the judges?' asked Junior.

Krishna shushed Junior. Turning to GGP, he said, 'It would not affect the banks, right? They would simply lower the interest on deposits, which means future investors would bear the cost of the bank's sins. What a travesty of fairness to the depositor!'

For a moment, even Senior was stumped. Sensing a win, Krishna remarked with an air of finality, 'If the bank bites the bullet, it will hurt its present shareholders. Whichever way, it is the citizens who pay for it!' He turned triumphantly to his cousin, smirking.

Junior had to bring all of his Harvard skills to the fore. 'This is not pandemic-specific. In the last 10 years, the interest rates at which banks borrow have fallen. So have the rates at which they lend. When they borrow, borrowers want as low a rate as is possible. When a crisis looms large, they want to reschedule both interest and principal repayment. It is a part of the genes of several borrowers!' He added, 'Anyway, if the account becomes an NPA, the borrowers will want a massive "haircut" to reduce payment.'

'A haircut? What is that?' asked Krishna, pushing back his growing clutch of hair.

Junior gave a satisfied smile, with the scale tilting in his favour. 'Borrowers try to get a one-time settlement with hefty write-offs from banks. Meaning, if I owe you ₹10,000, I tell you let's settle it for ₹6,000. Here, I am suggesting a 40 per cent haircut. You and I would call it discount, but the finance guys have their jargon.'

'So, if you pay me nothing, you are getting my head shaved?'

Both Senior and Junior laughed, leaving Krishna puzzled. He asked, 'GGP, but how did all this come to pass?'

Senior stood up to his full height of 6 feet 1 inches. It was an indication that it was time for tea. 'After tea, I plan to go for a stroll. If you guys feel up to it, you can join me, and I will answer your questions. Meanwhile, you Google two things: a note titled "The Arithmetic behind interest income", and an article headlined "Banks play footsy with recognizing losses", which appeared in a business paper in the winter of 2021. By the way, I forgot to tell you, M. Narasimham, career banker who became RBI governor, was the one who spearheaded the banking reforms in the 1990s.'

'Will do,' chorused the two.

Senior proudly said that the article received a million views.

Krishna scribbled the **LESSON**: When customers don't pay, banks cannot recognize income from the loan. When they cannot repay, banks have to take a haircut and square off the loan.

◆

That afternoon when the three of them stepped out to the neighbourhood park for a walk, Senior was in his pajamas. He wore a smartwatch that would instantly send a notification to his doctor if he faced any health issue.

'GGP, the news says that the NBH evergreened loans. What is evergreening?' Krishna asked.

Junior jumped in with an explanation. 'Let's say the cook takes a loan of ₹10,000 from Larissa Ma-Ma (short for grandmother). She promises to repay the loan in 10 months. She has paid seven installments, and everything is going smoothly. In the eighth month, she asks Larissa Ma-Ma for another ₹5,000. Ma-Ma asks her to first settle the older loan, to which the cook suggests that she give her ₹5,000, and from that, she will pay ₹3,000. That's called evergreening.'

Krishna looked at his cousin in admiration. 'Well put.'

Senior added, 'Evergreening is the practice where banks revive a loan on the verge of default by granting a further loan to the same borrower, so that the borrower can repay the first loan partially from the money from the second loan. Banks do that to stop the account from turning into an NPA. This practice puts lenders at risk of massive amounts of defaults, so the RBI disapproves of it.'

Krishna nodded sagely at the explanation. He then asked, 'Do you think I should know anything more about NPA?'

Senior was pleased at the boy's curiosity. 'Yes, there is one other important point. NPA computation is arithmetic and is done by the bank. But there are instances of divergence. The banks declare a certain sum as NPA, but the RBI inspectors come up with a different number.

'Yes Bank, State Bank of India (SBI), Punjab National Bank (PNB), Bank of India, Central Bank of India, Indian Bank, Indian Overseas Bank, Lakshmi Vilas Bank (LVB), UCO Bank and Union Bank of India have been equally guilty of divergence over the years.'

They had finished one round of the park. 'Another day, I will tell you about regulatory forbearance. It relates to laxity in the role of the RBI in supervision, oversight and enforcement of laws.'

Krishna wrote in his notepad. **LESSON:** How did so many banks fail to accurately compute their NPA figures? Was it intentional? Should ask some bankers.

THE ARITHMETIC BEHIND INTEREST INCOME

The central bank has laid out norms for income recognition, asset classification and provisioning for bank advances.

Income recognition is about when to recognize interest as income. Asset classification is to break down advances into performing and non-performing assets. Provisioning involves debiting a certain amount to the profit and loss account in order to be prudent in recognizing uncertain income.

Income recognition is formula-driven and based on the recovery record of the customer. There is no room for subjective considerations. The same goes for the classification of assets as also for provisioning.

Non-Performing Assets

An asset becomes non-performing when it ceases to earn income for the bank.

Generally, an NPA is an advance where the interest or installment remains 'overdue' for more than 90 days. An account is 'overdue' if an amount payable under the facility is not paid on the due date. Similarly, timelines have been laid out for overdrafts, bills, facilities backed by the central or state government, projects under implementation, advances against deposits, etc. As a rule of thumb, if a customer's facility with a bank is considered an NPA, then all borrowing of that customer with that bank will be treated as an NPA. Fair or unfair, that's the law.

If an account becomes an NPA, the entire interest credited to the income account in the past periods should be reversed if it has not been realized. The same goes for fees, commission and similar income.

Asset Classification

The NPAs are classified into substandard assets, doubtful assets and loss assets.

An asset that is not an NPA is called a standard asset. As the related RBI circular states, 'Banks are required to classify nonperforming assets further into the following three categories based on the period for which the asset has remained nonperforming and the realisability of the dues.'[7]

Assets	NPA period
Substandard Assets	NPA for less than or equal to 12 months
Doubtful Assets—D1	NPA for 12–24 months
Doubtful Assets—D2	NPA for 24–48 months
Doubtful Assets—D3	NPA for > 48 months
Loss Assets	Identified as unrecoverable by the bank, auditors or RBI inspectors.

Provisioning Norms

Based on the category of asset, a percentage of the outstanding loan has to be debited to the profit and loss account by the bank. For instance, if a loan to Mr X is outstanding for ₹200 lakh, and is a substandard asset, a provision of 15 per cent of ₹200 lakh, namely ₹30 lakh, has to be made in the bank's profit and loss account. To that extent, the profit will become lower.

NPA category	Provision
Substandard (Secured)	15 per cent of net outstanding
Substandard (Unsecured)	25 per cent of net outstanding

---

[7]Master Circulars, Reserve Bank of India, https://bit.ly/3TOq0NW. Accessed on 16 November 2022.

Doubtful I (Fully secured by Realisable Value of Security [RVS])	25 per cent of net outstanding
Doubtful I (Partly secured by RVS)	25 per cent of RVS plus 100 per cent of the unsecured portion
Doubtful II (Fully secured by RVS)	40 per cent of net outstanding
Doubtful II (Partly secured by RVS)	40 per cent of RVS plus 100 per cent of unsecured part
Doubtful III	100 per cent of net outstanding
Loss asset	100 per cent of net outstanding
Standard Assets	Ranging from 0.1 to 1 per cent, based on the type of advance

There are specific rules for providing doubtful assets if they have an ECGC (ECGC Ltd, formerly known as Export Credit Guarantee Corporation of India Ltd) guarantee, CGTMSE (Credit Guarantee Fund Trust for Micro and Small Enterprises) guarantee, etc.

BANKS PLAY FOOTSY WITH RECOGNIZING LOSSES

In India, there are various estimates of bad loans. One estimate places ₹10 lakh crore worth of loans as NPAs.[8] This translates to more than 10 per cent of all loans given. When restructured and unrecognized NPAs are added to this vast sum, the total stress comes to around 22–25 per cent of total loans.

Having to face such big hits, any banking system is bound to suffer.

This is not just a cloud that will pass with a rising gale. Nor is it a wound that can be covered with a Band-Aid. Various therapeutic treatments or significant surgical interventions are required. Also necessary is to understand why NPAs occur in the first place.

The prime reasons for NPAs include economic slowdown, a flawed credit appraisal process, inadequate post-disbursal monitoring, diversion of funds by promoters, improper valuations of securities, delayed reporting of frauds, rampant corruption, political intervention in the grant of loans and the wait-and-watch approach of banks. Besides these, the fear of the courts and the 3Cs—Central Bureau of Investigation (CBI), Central Vigilance Commission (CVC) and office of the Comptroller and Auditor General of India (CAG)—also play a role in the timing of NPA's recognition. That is, if there are high NPAs, questions tend to arise on why the loan was given, what were the considerations for giving the same, etc. So, the idea was to keep them standard by being within the four corners of law.

High NPAs have adversely affected the decisions made regarding fresh credit. An increasing number of bad loans have prompted banks to be ultra-cautious, shying away from even genuine lending, and this has significantly impacted India's economic activity.

World economies are reeling under the impact of the Covid-19 pandemic. Most businesses, particularly tourism, hospitality, amusement parks, theatres, the auto industry and aviation, among others, have

---

[8]Chopra, Amarjit, and Sabyasachee Dash, 'The NPA Conundrum', *The Statesman*, 30 November 2020, https://bit.ly/3AfFqne. Accessed on 16 November 2022.

been severely hit while many units face closures. If we want to revive business, we must sanction credit expeditiously. However, as bankers are scared of business decisions being subjected to subsequent scrutiny from auditors and inspectors of the RBI, they are cagey about taking decisions.

Resolving NPAs

There are two components that are vital in resolving NPAs: one, the immediate job of finding the banks' current accumulation; and, two, the more important long-term task of ensuring NPAs do not accumulate to this extent.

The main reason for the accumulation of bad loans is unrealistic growth expectations and overambitious projections that are eagerly accepted by lending institutions. This makes banks disburse credit left, right and centre. If the high expectations do not materialize, bad loans accumulate.

Let's look at this in another way. Banks finance a good portion of any healthy GDP. If the GDP keeps growing, the loan repayment does not get affected. But when the GDP growth tapers, the higher interest rates, inflation and exchange-rate fluctuations lead to many of these loans turning bad.

Banking-related skills, such as appraisal and monitoring skills of staff, adoption of technology, appreciation of borrower's genuine needs, size of the bank, pricing of loans, decision-making concerning restructuring, risk identification and mitigation measures taken, long-term strategy and capital adequacy also contribute to the accumulation of bad loans. Credit policy and the 'herd behaviour' of banks also play a role in the growth of NPAs.

Reporting and Rajan

The jump in NPAs during the 2010s can be attributed to the RBI. Indian banks had been under-reporting NPAs by a mile, with interbank transactions camouflaging the fundamental nature of the problem.

Added to that was rolling over existing loans to make their balance sheets look cleaner than they were. Therefore, official NPA figures on the banks' balance sheets did not represent the gravity of the issue.

When Raghuram G. Rajan, an Indian Institute of Technology (IIT)-Indian Institute of Management (IIM) alumnus and World Bank economist, came on the scene as RBI governor in 2013, he began the process of cleaning the Augean stables. Eight months into Prime Minister Narendra Modi's term, Rajan gave the PMO a list of high-profile cases that needed coordinated investigation.

In 2015, the highly respected governor ordered an Asset Quality Review, following which declared NPAs in banks spiked up to about ₹10 lakh crore.[9] The government took it in the right spirit, and followed 4Rs, namely, 'Recognize, Recapitalize, Recover and Reform'. Over the years, this helped quell the storm.

A year later, the government passed the landmark Insolvency and Bankruptcy Code (IBC), 2016.

After Rajan demitted office in 2016, the Parliamentary Committee on Estimates headed by Dr Murali Manohar Joshi wanted his views on bank NPA.[10] The former laid the origin of the crisis at the feet of the United Progressive Alliance-II, when economic growth was super strong.[11]

Rajan said, 'It is at such times that banks make mistakes,' and pointed to the fear of investigation paralysing government decision-making. On the National Democratic Alliance, he wrote, 'The continuing travails of the stranded power plants [...] suggest government decision making has not picked up sufficient pace to date.'[12]

[9]Chopra, Aamarjit, and Sabyasachee Dash, 'The NPA Conundrum', *The Statesman*, 30 November 2020, https://bit.ly/3WLRV2y. Accessed on 26 December 2022.

[10]'Full Text of Raghuram Rajan's Note to Parliamentary Estimates Committee on Bank NPAs', *The Indian Express*, 11 September 2018, https://bit.ly/3I2a34h. Accessed on 26 December 2022.

[11]Rajesh, Y.P., 'It All Began under UPA: Raghuram Rajan Gives Modi Ammunition against Congress on Bad Loans', *ThePrint*, 11 September 2018, https://bit.ly/3tzTUe8. Accessed on 16 November 2022.

[12]Rajan, Raghuram, 'Note to Parliamentary Estimates Committee on Bank NPAs', 6 September 2018, https://bit.ly/2N9uWun. Accessed on 27 October 2022.

However, what really stands out is his remark on penultimate preparedness. Peter Lynch explains the idea his book, *One Up on Wall Street*.[13] He writes:

> In Mayan Mythology, the universe was destroyed four times. Every time the Mayans learnt a sad lesson and vowed to be better protected, but it was always for the previous menace. First, there was a flood, and the survivors moved into the woods and put their houses in the trees. Their efforts went for naught because the world was destroyed by fire the next time.
>
> After that, the fire survivors ran as far away from the woods as possible. They built new houses out of stone. Soon an earthquake destroyed the world. I don't remember the fourth bad thing that happened, but whatever it was, the Mayans were going to miss it, busy building shelters for the next earthquake.

Rajan said, tongue firmly in cheek, that the 'government should focus on [the] sources of the next crisis, not just the last one'.[14]

Yes, we should not become a victim of penultimate preparedness.

[13]Lynch, Peter, and John Rothchild, *One Up on Wall Street: How to Use What You Already Know to Make Money in the Market*, Simon & Schuster, 2000, pp. 86–87.
[14]'Raghuram Rajan Red-Flags Mudra Scheme Loans as Possible Source of Next Banking Crisis', *Business Today*, 11 September 2018, https://bit.ly/3GgcXBD. Accessed on 16 November 2022.

4

MULTIPLE BALANCE SHEET PROBLEMS

They were now in for a second stroll of the day. Senior was ready for his stroll post-tea, in sneakers and a T-shirt, while Junior, now taller than Senior, wore shorts, a half-sleeved shirt and Adidas shoes. Krishna took his cycle and decided to ride along at the pace the others walked.

'Hey, what are you up to?' asked Junior.

'I can ride as fast or slow as you walk,' declared the young one.

Senior burst out laughing, amused by his fourth-generation ward. 'So, what was your question before we broke for tea?'

'I wanted to know how all of this came about.'

'Well, to get to that, you have to go back in time. We must go to the mid-2010s. At that time, our GDP growth had begun to slide, and there were even doubts about the government's data on GDP.'

'What's GDP?' Krishna slowed down his cycle.

'GDP refers to gross domestic product. This is the market value of all the final goods and services produced in a year. In a way, we can say that it is the total wealth that a country creates during a period.' Junior was in lecture mode, much to Krishna's displeasure.

Senior nodded in agreement. 'India had generally grown at 8 per cent earlier. The fall in the second half of the 2010s was so drastic that economists started saying that the nation was heading towards the intensive care unit.

'A gentleman called Arvind Subramanian was India's chief economic advisor, or CEA, at the time. A St Stephen's economics graduate, he later went on to study at IIM-A and Oxford.

'Officially, the CEA is head of Economic Division of the Department of Economic Affairs, Government of India. One of his responsibilities is to produce the annual Economic Survey. The Survey reviews the economic development in India over the previous year, analyses the country's macroeconomics and provides an outline for the next financial year.

'Subramanian first discussed what he called the "twin balance sheet challenge" in the Economic Survey of 2016–17. Within the next couple of years, the twin balance sheet crisis became "triple balance sheet problem", and later a "four balance sheet catastrophe".'

By this time Krishna had got down from his cycle and was pushing it along. A little tentative, knowing he would get a mouthful from his cousin, he asked, 'But what is a balance sheet?'

Junior was in a good mood. He explained, 'It is a statement of your assets and liabilities. Assets are what you own, and liabilities are what you owe.'

'Hmm…'

His cousin continued. 'Remember GGP had said about your lending me ₹10,000?'

'Yeah.'

'When you lend, it continues to be money that you own. It, therefore, appears as an asset in your balance sheet. It is money that I owe and therefore appears as a liability in my balance sheet.'

'Well, you seem to have a nice way of explaining,' said Krishna. Junior was not sure if the appreciation was genuine or sarcastic.

Ignoring him, Junior asked Senior, 'But what is the twin balance sheet problem?'

'You told Brat about your balance sheet and his balance sheet. If there is a problem in both, it becomes a twin balance sheet problem.'

'I am sort of getting that. But how does it happen, and is it interconnected?' asked Junior

'Of course, it is interconnected. For example, if you do not return the money you borrowed from Brat, and if that amount was significant, he will have a problem on the asset side of his balance sheet. He is saddled with unrecoverable debt.

'And you are unable to pay because you have a problem with your earnings. So, you, too, have a problem with your balance sheet. Since both Brat and you have problems in your respective balance sheets, it came to be called the twin balance sheet problem.'

Junior suddenly saw a flash of light in the dark tunnel. 'So, in real life, Brat is "Brat Bank", and I am "Corporate India". Right?'

'You couldn't have put it better. The bank had a problem in its balance sheet, and corporate India had one in its balance sheet too.'

'And then a third entity came in to make it a triple balance sheet crisis, and still later a fourth to make it a four balance sheet disaster. And it happened fast. Am I right?'

'Absolutely! When banks couldn't lend, they got the non-banking financial companies, or NBFCs, to do so. These NBFCs came to be called shadow banks and lent money to real estate companies. They were the third entity. When the real estate market slumped, both the NBFCs and the real estate companies were saddled with rotten eggs or a bad balance sheet. So, now we had a four balance sheet issue.'

'That's wonderful!' said Junior. 'You must have written about this somewhere? Why don't you pass it on to us when we return from our walk?'

'Ha, it is there on my mobile. I will forward it to you both right away. You can read it up before we meet the next time.'

Krishna texted himself. **LESSON**: From two balance sheet, the crisis grew into a four balance sheet catastrophe. Banks, corporates, lenders and real estate companies were in deep shit.

He would be in trouble if the adults read the last word but felt that it appropriately described the situation.

TWIN BALANCE SHEETS AND OTHER STORIES

A twin balance sheet problem arose due to two factors: (a) India's over-leveraged companies and (b) bad loan-saddled public sector banks.

During the early 2000s, India Inc. helped itself to a lot of readily available credit from state-run banks and accumulated disproportionate debt. The moment environmental clearances by the government started getting delayed and financing costs began to rise, debt servicing became a challenge.

Lower revenue, higher costs and greater interest charge squeezed corporate India. By 2013, companies with an interest coverage ratio of less than one owed one-third of corporate debt. Many of them were in the infrastructure, particularly in the power-generation sector. The interest coverage ratio measures how much money is available in order to pay off the interest. It is calculated by dividing the firm's EBIT (earnings before interest and taxes) by its interest expense during a period. Some variations of the formula use EBITDA (earnings before interest, taxes, depreciation and amortization) or EBIAT (earnings before interest after taxes) instead of EBIT to calculate the ratio. A higher coverage ratio is better.

The Trouble with Banks

The failure of infrastructure companies to service debt caused rising overdue in bank balance sheets. 'More than four-fifths of the non-performing assets were in the public sector banks, where the NPA ratio reached almost 12 percent,' said *The Economic Survey.*[15]

This made banks more cautious when lending. The resultant NPA problem made the RBI lay down more stringent classification norms, and subsequently, several state-run banks came under the central banker's Prompt Corrective Action (PCA) norms.

---

[15]Singh, Garima, 'What Arvind Subramanian Meant When He Talked of India's Four Balance Sheet Challenge', *The Economic Times*, 24 December 2019, https://bit.ly/3GhXS2j. Accessed on 16 November 2022.

Triple Balance Sheet Problem

When banks refrained from lending so as to contain NPAs, they turned to NBFCs for support, boosting both investment and private consumption. And then the impossible happened in September 2018. That month, Infrastructure Leasing & Financial Services (IL&FS) collapsed, sending shockwaves across the country. Its failure to service debt started a chain of events and accelerated the bank's ability to lend money.

With NBFCs choking, the twin balance sheet problem expanded to become the triple balance sheet problem. Corporates, banks and now NBFCs—three choking balance sheets—set up the textbook case for a cardiac arrest.

The Four Balance Sheet Challenge

In his paper titled 'India's Great Slowdown', Subramanian mentioned the 'Four balance sheet challenge',[16] which includes infrastructure companies and banks as well as NBFCs and real estate companies.

When IL&FS, which carried a debt of ₹90,000 crore, fell, the markets finally woke up to address the issue. 'What the markets discovered was profoundly disturbing. Much of the NBFC lending had been channeled to one particular sector, real estate. And that sector itself was in a precarious situation,' wrote Subramanian.

NBFCs were a significant participant in financing the real estate sector's growth. The paper said, 'Historically the bulk of formal sector real estate funding was provided by banks, but in recent years most of the incremental lending has come from NBFCs, so much so that by 2018–19, NBFCs accounted for about half of the ₹5 lakh crore in real estate loans outstanding.'

However, when the demand started to fall, servicing debt became difficult for the builders, and NBFC balance sheets started to cave,

---

[16]Subramanian Arvind, and Josh Felman, 'India's Great Slowdown: What Happened? What's the Way Out?' CID Faculty Working Paper No. 370, Center for International Development at Harvard University, December 2019, https://bit.ly/3DB4R4B. Accessed on 27 October 2022.

leading to a four balance sheet problem.

Subramanian argued, 'In this situation [...] monetary policy cannot revive the economy because the transmission mechanism is broken. Fiscal policy cannot be used because the financial system would have difficulty absorbing the large bond issues that a stimulus would entail. The traditional structural reform agenda—land and labor market measures—will not address the current problems.'

He gave a six-point action plan.

1. Launch a new asset quality review to cover banks and NBFCs (Recognition)
2. Make changes to the IBC to better align incentives (Resolution)
3. Create two executive-led public sector asset restructuring companies ('bad banks'), one each for the real estate and power sectors (Resolution)
4. Strengthen oversight, especially of NBFCs (Regulation)
5. Link recapitalization to resolution (Recapitalization)
6. Shrink public sector banking (Reform)[17]

When Subramanian left one year into his second term to pursue his interest in academia, the then finance minister Arun Jaitley complimented his work, saying the former's early diagnosis of the twin balance sheet crisis led to the government outlining higher public investment in the Budget.[18]

[17]Ibid. 27-28.

[18]'Arvind Subramanian Quits. Five Things for Which Arun Jaitley Lauded Him', NDTV, 20 January 2018, https://bit.ly/3g40Zk0. Accessed on 16 November 2022.

5

HOW BANKS MAKE PROFITS: PART 1

The patriarch turned to his two wards and said, 'Today, we will talk about the one factor that can kill a company, including banks. And surprisingly, that's the very factor that can also magnify a company's return.'

Krishna was quick on the uptake. 'You mean like a double-edged sword, GGP?'

'Absolutely,' said the 89-year-old Senior, adjusting imaginary hair on his head.

'Junior, what I am going to talk about today may not be new for you, but for Krishna, it will be an instructive lesson.'

'But, GGP, when you explain, my understanding becomes more concrete. You can expect me to pay full attention to whatever you say.'

'Butter. Butter,' said Krishna, eliciting a ferocious look from Junior.

Krishna wore a hangdog expression and asked, 'What has leverage got to do in finance? The only leverage that I know about is in physics.'

'So, what is it you know?' asked Senior.

'Load multiplied with load arm equals effort multiplied with effort arm,' said Krishna.

Junior couldn't help but smile. And so did Senior. 'That's absolutely right. Please elaborate.'

'Over 2,000 years ago, Archimedes stated that, given a lever long enough and a fulcrum on which to place it, he could move the earth.'

'And you believed that, Brat?' taunted Junior. 'The crux of the matter is that small forces can move great weights using a lever.'

'Yes, yes. There are three elements in the lever: fulcrum, the one that causes the movement and the one that is moved. The greater the distance from the fulcrum, the more easily it will move.' Krishna spoke from memory, and Junior could not help but dissolve into laughter.

Senior patted the furious Krishna on his back and said, 'He is amazed at the technical knowledge you have.'

It made Krishna smile. 'I can give another example. The Egyptians used levers to lift stones weighing 100 tonnes.'

'That's good. Now, Junior, can you help us understand what leverage in finance is? I am sure in your class at Harvard, you read about how it can both help and destroy companies.'

Junior was unprepared, but the 140-IQ lad rose to his full height and said, 'In finance, leverage is the introduction of debt into a company's business. The money that owners bring in is called equity and is "risk capital".

'Companies also raise loans. There are several reasons, the chief being that loans are cheaper. The lenders charge interest on these loans, and this interest payment is tax deductible.

'Since interest and repayment are guaranteed, debt is a less risky investment option for the lender. Hence, he is fine with a lower return. Remember, in investments, return is directly proportional to risk. Now, because raising debt is cheaper than equity, debt magnifies the return on equity.'

Krishna had a sparkle in his eyes. 'You mean equity is money that I have earned and so is my own money, while debt is what I have borrowed from you, right?'

'Absolutely!'

'Numbers. Numbers. Please walk me through numbers; I can't make much out of sentences.' The son of a banker had to be a banker. After all, banking ran in the genes, Krishna McKenzie's avowed claims of wanting to study engineering notwithstanding.

In any case, many IIT boys end up either on Wall Street or Dalal Street.

Senior walked up to the magnetic whiteboard that he had placed on the wall of his study room. Scribbling some numbers, he said, 'Suppose the company A Ltd has ₹1,000 as equity. A Ltd invests this amount in, say, advances that earn 15 per cent. This means the company makes ₹1,000 × 15 per cent, that is ₹150. For the sake of simplicity, let us assume there is no tax. So, the post-tax earning is ₹150. The equity shareholder invested ₹1,000, and hence his return is 150/1,000, i.e., 15 per cent.'

Junior turned to Krishna and asked, 'Are you with him?'

'Yes, yes. Go on, GGP. Isn't that obvious?' Krishna was scribbling in his notepad.

'Yes, but bear with me. Now, assume this company has ₹400 as debt and ₹600 as equity. This is a debt–equity ratio of 2:3. So, 40 per cent of its funds is in equity, and it's called 40 per cent leverage. Going with the above example, the company invests in advances that earn 15 per cent. This means the company still makes ₹150.' Senior now took a deep breath

The grand old man was happy with Krishna. Everyone believed he was destined for greater things, especially as he was the sole survivor that crazy night when a speeding lorry hit their car.

Senior's thoughts came back to the present. 'Let us assume that debt holders charge 11 per cent. So, they will have to be paid ₹400 × 11 per cent = ₹44. Considering no tax, the after-tax earnings for the company are ₹150—₹44 = ₹106. This ₹106 belongs to the equity shareholders. These men had invested ₹600, so the return on equity is 106/600, namely 17.66 per cent. Notice that while the productivity of money, technically called the return on capital employed, continues to be 15 per cent, the return to equity shareholders goes up to 17.66 per cent.'

'So, the return has increased from 15 per cent to 17.66 per cent.'

Junior said, 'As we keep increasing the proportion of debt in the capital, equity shareholders' returns keep rising. This is the beautiful advantage of borrowing—'

Krishna interrupted him, saying, 'Let's have a glass of water, refocus and then you can resume.'

'Are you getting tired?' asked Junior.

'No, I am excited. Like you stop before you turn to the next page of a mystery novel, I want to take a deep breath and savour the moment.'

After a brief break of a couple of minutes, Senior started explaining the impact of taxation in this scenario. 'In our example, suppose the tax rate is 25 per cent. When the company was an all-equity firm, it earned a profit before tax of ₹150, for which the tax will be ₹37.5. If we deduct this amount, the company is left with ₹112.5. The return to equity shareholders is now 11.25 per cent. I am sure you have now understood the computations.'

Junior took over. 'When the company has 40 per cent leverage, it earned a profit before tax of ₹106, for which the tax will be ₹26.5, leaving it with an after-tax profit of ₹79.5. The return to equity shareholders is now 79.5/600 = 13.25 per cent.

'The tax example shows how introducing debt into the capital structure magnifies the return on equity.' And he rounded it off saying, 'Companies ramp up debt in their capital for a few reasons, such as (a) debt being cheaper than equity, (b) the interest payment is tax-deductible, and (c) helping shareholders obtain a bigger bang for their buck.'

Krishna scratched his head with his pen and looked at the far corner of the room. It was an indication that he would come up with a wild question. He didn't disappoint. 'But is it all summer and sunshine? All that a company must do to increase the return to its shareholders is to add more leverage to its capital?'

Both Senior and Junior were taken aback by the question coming from a 13-year-old. The former said, 'Now, that's an excellent question. It is not all summer and sunshine. There is thunder and sandstorm as well. 'We earlier saw that leverage is good because it helps us magnify the return to shareholders. Like you said, business organizations could be tempted to use plenty of debt to magnify the return on equity. Let's now understand how this can be risky.

'Suppose, A Ltd has ₹1,000 as equity. It has invested this amount in, say, advances. Assume that 20 per cent of the advances go bad. The company loses ₹200. The equity shareholder has invested ₹1,000, his loss is ₹200, or 20 per cent.'

Krishna was fully attentive and yet, at the same time, scribbling rapidly.

Senior was in full flow. 'Next, assume this company has ₹400 as debt and ₹600 as equity. Going with the above example, the company invests ₹1,000, and say about 20 per cent go bad, so, the company loses ₹200. Because the debt holders are guaranteed their interest and principal, this loss is borne entirely by equity shareholders. These guys had given ₹600, and now ₹200 is lost. Therefore, their loss is 33 per cent. Introducing debt increased their loss from 20 per cent to 33 per cent, even as the overall business's risk was the same. We call this shareholders' risk.'

As Senior fussed over the hot coffee served to him, Junior explained, 'As we keep increasing the proportion of debt in the capital, equity shareholders' risk keeps rising. Do your little math today. You will find that if the debt–equity ratio is 1:1, and if 20 per cent of the total advance of ₹1,000 is lost, shareholders' risk is ₹200/500, or 40 per cent. More debt keeps increasing the percentage of loss.'

A smiling Krishna extended his left hand, asking his cousin to stop. He then said, 'If the leverage is 99:1 and one ₹1 of advance goes bad, the equity shareholders have lost their entire capital. The risk is 100 per cent. Right?'

Both Junior and Senior gave Krishna a standing ovation.

'Ha! I now understand what you meant in your article that we read yesterday about over-leveraged banks,' said Krishna.

The little one had already noted his **LESSON:** Leverage is a double-edged sword. It can magnify returns when the going is good but kill if things turn terrible.

Peeping slyly into the notes, Junior said, 'For many highly levered companies, the going turned awful.'

WHY BANKS FAIL: IS PRIVATIZATION THE ANSWER?

Rural branches have historically been running at a loss due to high overheads, large loan waivers and rising NPAs. Priority sector lending is viewed as a social obligation instead of a bottom-of-the-pyramid business model. Banks are losing out to financial intermediaries when mobilizing deposits. Mutual funds, housing finance corporations and private sector banks take the cream away by paying better interest rates. Finally, there has been a lot of political pressure regarding lending.

Privatization of banks was often provided as one of the possible solutions. The argument is that businessmen will focus on profitability, while governments focus on social welfare. However, privatization is not really the answer, as later on hurdles surface.

The stories of Global Trust Bank in the 2000s, Yes Bank in the 2010s and LVB in the 2020s tell you that private banks, too, do not necessarily fare better than public sector banks. This is true globally. Lehman Brothers in the United States (US) was a private bank that collapsed in 2008. Also, when it comes to divergence, both private and public sector banks are equally guilty.

The government inherited an NPA problem of massive magnitude. Following this, the amount of bad loans written off from 2014 to 2020 was ₹660,000 crore.[19] NPAs are not exclusively generated in public sector banks. There are also reports of divergence between the NPAs

[19]Sharma, Pulkit, 'Banks Wrote Off ₹6,60,000 Crore Worth Bad Loans Since Modi Came to Power', NewsClick, 15 March 2020, https://bit.ly/3tADVfA. Accessed on 16 November 2022.

disclosed by private sector banks and unearthed by RBI inspectors, as with Axis Bank and ICICI Bank.[20] Ownership, public or private, may not have much impact on this aspect of a bank's functioning. What does in fact have an impact is how effectively the regulator works. Strengthening regulatory controls and improving governance rather than changing the ownership structure will have a real effect on reducing fraud.

India's mounting bad debt problem is partly due to crony capitalism, where political opportunism plays a big hand. A lot of electoral mileage has been availed by political parties in this regard. There have been charges of calls coming in from the higher-ups suggesting loans be given.[21]

The loan melas were part of priority sector lending, which the government of the day wanted the public sector banks to carry out. The concept owes its origin to economist D.R. Gadgil, then deputy chairman of the Planning Commission, whose 1969 report propounded it. The political class liked the idea as it was a convenient tool to promote populism among vote banks. Political leaders attend such melas where public sector banks are given targets to distribute crores. Alas, it added to the portfolio of NPAs as the loans were granted without due diligence. Borrowers stop repayments for such loans knowing that the politicians themselves will call for waiving these loans during elections to appease the voters.

Actually, public sector banks have done a great job of financial inclusion. When it comes to rural coverage, they have done better than private players. As of 1 April 2021, public sector banks had close to 44,397 rural branches (84 per cent of the total rural branches), while private sector banks had only 8,235 rural branches, with a

[20]Lele, Abhijit, 'RBI Tightens Disclosure Norms on Divergence in NPAs, Provisions', *Business Standard*, 11 October 2022, https://bit.ly/3twSMI0. Accessed on 16 November 2022.

[21]'Bank Union Opposes Public Sector Banks' 'Loan Melas' on NPA Pile-Up Fears', *Business Standard*, 5 September 2022, https://bit.ly/3txn514. Accessed on 16 November 2022.

16 per cent rural share.[22]

The way forward is to carry out better regulations and control mechanisms.

Some believe that public sector banks are lax because they know the government will step in as a white knight to save them. This is counterintuitive. Mark it; the CEO will still have to serve prison time, even if he enjoys political patronage.

To win, what the banking system needs are: (a) Complete autonomy to the PSU banks from the government, (b) Strict regulation by the RBI, (c) Board independent of people with political leanings, and (d) Performance-based pay for the bankers.

The government must not sell its share in banks but look at alternatives. A bank comes with physical assets, stock portfolio, brand name, human resource and customer base, among other things. Today, buyers do not want the entire business of the bank because their interests do not lie in every part of the bank. A North-based branch without a Southern presence would be interested in physical branches, like what happened when DBS took over LVB. However, if a bank already has adequate physical presence, it will be interested only in the customer and not in the branch building.

Some players will be interested in physical branches and will be ready to pay a premium. For example, a real estate company will be interested in the building and not the bank's business. So, it makes sense to segregate business from building and sell them separately. Others will be willing to buy the bank's brand name. Some may be interested in the workforce or in the customers. Real estate developers will be keen on land and buildings. Portfolio managers may angle for the portfolio investment. So, the most practical approach would be to create tranches and sell each tranche to the best bidder on a valuation model, instead of selling the entire bank as an entity.

[22]Rao, PSM, 'Why The Government Should Not Bank on Privatisation', *Deccan Herald*, 1 April 2021, https://bit.ly/3ObYnwL. Accessed on 16 November 2022.

6

HOW BANKS MAKE PROFITS: PART 2

Lobin Stephen Senior and his two great-grandsons sat on the sprawling lawn of their house, despite the chilly weather. Senior layered two sweaters, Junior had a blazer on and Krishna showed up in a striped T-shirt. Krishna kept his index finger on his lips, indicating to Junior that he would not offer any comment on his attire. While he stood on the moist grass, the other two were seated in a chair. On a small table lay small hot samosas.

'Today, let's talk about how banks make profits, and how in their attempt at doing so, they end up stacking bad loans,' said Senior.

'Is there anything substantial to discuss?' asked Krishna. 'After all, they raise money at a lower rate and then lend at a higher rate. That's typical moneylending business.'

'You are right about the broad mechanics. But there are several other rates, such as CRAR, SLR, CRR, etc., that we should know about,' Junior told his cousin.

Senior began in right earnest. 'A bank raises money through demand and time liabilities deposits. Demand liabilities are to be repaid whenever "demanded" by the depositors, while time liabilities are payable only upon maturity. Both these monies have a cost. The bank lends them at a higher rate to earn a spread. In other words, "spread" is the difference between the rate at which a bank lends and the rate at which it borrows. Against the spread, there are fixed operating expense, or OpEx, and the difference between spread and these costs is the bank's profit.'

Junior picked up a samosa and handed it over to his great-grandfather.

Krishna took this opportunity to rattle out some numbers. 'Tell me if I got it right? Suppose a bank raises ₹100 crore at 7 per cent and lends it at 11 per cent. Its margin is now 4 per cent, or ₹4 crore. If its OpEx is ₹3 crore, it makes a profit of ₹1 crore.'

'Perfect!' said Junior.

Thrilled at having had a word of appreciation from his fastidious cousin, Krishna turned towards Senior. In a stentorian voice, he said, 'Lobin Stephen Senior, should you really be eating oily samosas at this age?'

For a moment, the elderly man was taken aback. He gathered his wits to remark, 'I am in the pink of health: no diabetes, no hypertension, no cholesterol. No nothing.'

A smiling Krishna remarked, 'Then, you're too good to be true.'

'While your calculation is right, things do not work that easily in finance. For instance, if all the ₹100 crore are lent by the bank and one cloudy morning, customers start queuing up to take back their deposits, the bank will not have money to repay them. If there is even the slightest hint that the bank cannot return deposits, there will be a run on the bank. A "run" would mean more people queueing up to take their money back. The moral is: a part of the ₹100 crore *has* to be kept as liquid money.'

Just then Senior's phone rang. The screen showed 'private number'. He turned to Junior, asking him to take over the conversation while he took the call. Junior had already gone through 'Banking 101' in his first semester, so he was well equipped.

'The central bank requires banks to maintain two reserves, namely SLR and CRR.'

'What do they mean?' asked Krishna.

'Sorry! SLR is short for statutory liquidity ratio, while CRR is cash reserve ratio. Every bank has to keep a percentage of its assets as cash balance with the RBI. This is called CRR. Every bank must also invest a portion of NDTL in liquid assets. This is the statutory liquidity ratio. Liquid assets include gold, treasury bills, government-approved SLR securities and cash.

'Before you ask, NDTL is short for net demand and time liabilities. Demand liabilities are those that the bank needs to pay whenever the customer asks for them. Some examples include current deposits, demand drafts, overdue deposits and savings bank balance. Time liabilities will have to be repaid on maturity and where the depositor cannot usually withdraw ahead of time. Fixed deposit is another example.'

Impressed, Krishna said, 'You seem to know a lot about all this.'

His cousin gave him a wicked smile. 'I don't go to Harvard to make samosas!'

By now Senior had finished his call. Neither of his great-grandsons asked who the caller was. They had been taught never to poke their nose into other people's business. Krishna poured his great grandfather some tea into a porcelain cup.

'Let's get back to CRR and SLR. If the CRR is 5 per cent and the NDTL is ₹100 crore, the bank has to keep ₹5 crore as cash with the RBI,' said Senior.

'You mean this ₹5 crore has to be held with the central bank as free money, GGP?' Krishna added.

'Yes. It neither earns interest, nor is it available for lending. Similarly, if the SLR in that bank is 20 per cent, then ₹20 crore will have to be kept as liquid assets. But the good news is that the SLR money earns income for the bank because it is invested in liquid assets.'

'And it is not available for lending because the money cannot be in two places at the same time,' Krishna added.

Junior loved the choice of words and gave his cousin a thumbs up.

'That's not all,' continued Senior. 'You see, both CRR and SLR impact a bank's profitability as also its solvency.'

'You mean they lead to bad loans?' asked Junior.

'Yes. Let us go back to our initial example: the one about a bank that raises ₹100 crore deposits at 7 per cent, lends at 11 per cent and whose OpEx is 3 per cent. We said it made a profit of ₹1 crore.'

'So, what about it?' asked the two in unison.

'With CRR and SLR coming in, the economics changes. Notice that the cost of raising money is ₹7 crore (₹100 crore x 7 per cent), OpEx is ₹3 crore and the desired profit is ₹1 crore. Hence, the lender has to earn ₹11 crore. Because the CRR and SLR take away 25 per cent, the money available is only ₹75 crore, which the bank has to lend at 11/75 x 100, i.e., 14.67 per cent to make up this amount. So, the loans have to be given to lower-quality entities, which could lead to bad loans. Of course, this is not a justification for loans to go lemon.'

Junior had a flash of insight. 'And when bad loans surface, they affect the profits, and this forces banks to lend to worse customers at higher rates to try and shore up the bottom line. So, apart from the cost of pre-emption, the possibility of bad loans requires further increase in lending rates. In a way, good loans subsidize bad loans.'

'You could not have put it better,' remarked Senior. 'By the way, SLR and CRR funds are also called pre-empted funds. The required enhancement in lending rates is called the cost of pre-emption.'

'I think I need a break. This has been heavy stuff for me,' said Krishna, getting up without expecting his great grandfather to respond.

'I agree. Let's meet in half an hour,' remarked Junior.

'Meanwhile, please go through the article I have just forwarded to you on WhatsApp,' said Senior.

BANKS, INFLATION AND GROWTH

The RBI uses SLR and CRR to pump money into or suck money out of the banking system. That way, it regulates growth and inflation.

If the economy is stagnating, the RBI may want the banks to lend and corporates to invest in, say, capital expenditures capex. In such a situation, it would reduce the SLR or CRR percentage. This will increase the amount available for lending. On the flip side, the additional money can lead to inflation. And if there is too much inflation, the RBI might like to suck liquidity out of the market by increasing the CRR and SLR requirements. More money will now have to be invested by banks in these investments, and less money will be available for lending. This will affect economic growth but control inflation.

Managing the two—growth and inflation—is a perennial challenge for central bankers.

When the CRR is raised, the banks have to place more money with the RBI, and to that extent, their ability to lend comes down. Similarly, when the SLR is raised, the banks have to place more money in liquid assets, and so their loanable money reduces. Consequently, there will be less money to earn the cost of borrowing that they have incurred. Thus, the banks will increase their lending rates to catch up on the higher cost of funds. As interest rates go up, borrowing becomes expensive and inflation falls.

Another function of the CRR is to control interest rates. This is done by either increasing or reducing liquidity in the market. Too much liquidity leads to lower interest rates, while scarcity of money results in higher interest rates. Neither is healthy for the economy. So, when there is too much money in the market, the RBI increases the SLR, creating scarcity in the market and thus hardening the interest rate. Similarly, when there is too little money in the system, the RBI lowers the SLR, allowing money to come out of the banking pipeline, which reduces the interest rate.

Forty-five minutes later, the three were back on the lawn.

Junior was the first off the mark. 'The CRAR, or capital to risk weighted assets ratio, is something I don't understand. You should tell us about that.'

Senior's mind went back to 2008—the year of the global financial crisis, when several institutions went down the tubes. The world realized that banks should put more capital into their balance sheet and thus increase their ability to absorb bad loans.

In the early 2000s, bankers had lent indiscriminately and taken substantial off-balance-sheet exposures. These did not involve an immediate financial obligation, such as giving a letter of credit. Following this, banks were asked to recapitalize, and CRAR turned into a buzzword. Bank recapitalization meant infusing more capital or money in banks.

'Fine,' Senior said, coming out of his reverie. Turning to Krishna, he asked, 'Do you remember how banks make money?'

'Sure, sure. A bank raises money as equity and deposits, and lends in the form of loans. It has to keep some part of its money as SLR or CRR to meet "runs" on banks.'

Senior looked up, not very happy with what he heard, but he let that pass. He felt that the answer was inadequate. 'Remember, under SLR obligations, banks must invest in government securities. Each advance carries a different level of risk. For instance, staff loans carry 20 per cent risk, and credit card outstanding carry 100 per cent risk. Investments in government securities carry zero risk.'

The elderly man continued, taking in his great-grandsons' attentive faces. 'CRAR is the ratio of equity capital to risk weighted assets and measures how well a bank is capitalized about its assets. Let me run you through some numbers, so you understand the calculation and what it means. When out of ₹1,000 lakh, ₹250 lakh is in government securities, ₹350 lakh is in staff loans and ₹400 lakh is in credit card dues, the risk-weighted advance is ₹470 lakh. You can multiply the amount with the risk percentage for the calculation: $(0 \times 250 + 0.20 \times 350 + 1 \times 400)/1,000 = ₹470$ lakh. If the company has equity of ₹50 lakh, it would mean that the CRAR is $50/470 \times 100$, i.e., 10.6 per cent.'

'What is the acceptable CRAR?' It was Krishna, who was known to forever look for templates.

'Internationally, 8 per cent. In India, scheduled private sector banks must maintain 9 per cent, while public sector banks have to hold 12 per cent. If a bank has a higher CRAR, it is better capitalized.'

'What you are saying, GGP, is that in this case the debt–equity ratio is 950:50 or 19:1, and this is acceptable both in public sector banks and internationally as CRAR is 10.6 per cent?' asked Junior.

'Absolutely!'

'So, CRAR is basically the same as leverage?' asked Krishna.

'Good question,' said Senior. 'The CRAR isn't the debt–equity ratio, though we can look at it as one version of leverage. Let me scribble some numbers on the board to help both of you understand better. As you said, in the present case, it is okay to work at a debt–equity ratio of 19:1.

'Yet, if all ₹1,000 lakh had been credit card outstanding, the weighted asset would have been ₹1,000 lakh and the equity would have to be ₹106 lakh to have a CRAR of 10.6 per cent. This would have meant a debt–equity ratio of 904:106 = 8.52.

'So, in one case, a 19:1 debt–equity ratio translates into a CRAR of 10.6 per cent and in another case an 8.52:1 debt–equity ratio leads to a CRAR of 10.6 per cent. Hence, CRAR is a function of how the money is utilized, and bankers believe that this is a better indication of capitalization than the traditional debt–equity ratio.'

'I got it,' said Junior even as Krishna nodded thoughtfully, scratching his head again with his pencil—everything was still not fully clear for him. 'Debt–equity ratio signifies how the bank is funded, while the CRAR denotes the extent of financing of risky assets with equity.'

'That's well put,' remarked Senior.

Krishna quickly googled and read out, 'A few examples of risk weights assigned to various assets by the RBI are:

- 0 per cent: Cash, balance with the RBI, government-guaranteed advances
- 20 per cent: Secured loan to staff
- 50 per cent: Gold loans
- 75 per cent: Housing loans above ₹30 lakh
- 100 per cent: Consumer credit
- 125 per cent: Credit cards

'Off-balance sheet items, too, receive a conversion factor. For instance, letters of credit are at 20 per cent, unconditionally cancelable commitments 0 per cent, commitment with a maturity of one year is 20 per cent, etc.'

Saying so, Krishna started scribbling the **LESSON** in his notepad: CRAR is an extension of the leverage ratio, except that it focusses on the quality of lending. The minimum CRAR is expected to absorb the shock of bad loan losses.

Peeping into Krishna's notepad, Junior said, 'You could also make a note about Tier 1 and Tier 2 capital.'

Before Krishna could show his anger on Junior's continued intrusion, his cousin said, 'Tier 1 capital consists of shareholders' equity and retained earnings. Tier 2 capital includes revaluation reserves, hybrid capital instruments and subordinated term debt, general loan-loss reserves, and undisclosed reserves. These are important in deciding how well a bank is capitalized.'

Senior said, 'I am forwarding a note on a few other terms like repo and reverse repo. Once you read them up, you will have a complete understanding of how banks work. Do read it, because it will also tell you how each of these affect the economy. Let's take a few days' break now. You guys ruminate over what you learnt. Let's catch up in the New Year, on 2 January.'

THE RATE JOURNEY

It is important to know how banks raise money and how they lend. This will help us understand how it affects the economy.

When a bank is short of money, it goes to the RBI, which either gives a clean loan or one against security. The rate it charges for a clean loan is called the bank rate. The rate it levies when it takes security against a loan is called the repo rate, short for repurchase option rate. Obviously, the bank rate is higher than the repo rate, as there are no securities attached, and so the risk is higher.

The repo rate is so-called because of how the lending is done. The borrower bank first sells its securities to the RBI and immediately arranges to repurchase them at a higher price on a specified future date. The difference represents the interest. For instance, if it sells its security at ₹1,000 and agrees to repurchase it 15 days later for ₹1,005, the interest is ₹5. This is 0.5 per cent for the 15 days, that is, 12 per cent per annum. Repos are for a very short duration.

A higher repo rate suggests a higher cost of short-term money and a lower repo rate indicates a lower cost. If the borrowing cost is high, the bank will have to lend at a higher rate, which may slow down the economy. If the rate is low, banks can charge lower interest rates on their loans. This can speed up the GDP growth.

Incidentally, bank rate caters to commercial banks' long-term financial requirements, while repo rate focusses on short-term needs. Let's see how the RBI uses these two rates to monitor inflation and drive liquidity. If the RBI wants to improve liquidity, it reduces the repo rate and thus encourages banks to sell their securities. If it wants to curtail liquidity, it increases the interest rate, and so discourages banks from borrowing quickly.

MCLR and MCF

Before 2016, there was something called the base rate. This was the minimum rate at which banks could lend, and was based on the average cost of raising money, CRR, profit margin and Operating Expenses (aka OpEx). Various banks used different methods to compute the cost of capital and some did not pass on to the customers the rate cuts received from the RBI.

In 2016, marginal cost of funds-based lending rate (MCLR) was introduced. Banks were asked to pass on the benefit of the rate cut to borrowers.

The term 'marginal' refers to 'additional'. Here, marginal cost refers to the price of the marginal or additional money. There are four items that determine the MCLR.

The first is the cost of marginal funds (MCF), which is calculated by taking into account all the bank's borrowings. In computing the cost of capital, borrowing has a weight of 92 per cent, while the equity has 8 per cent weightage. This 8 per cent is equivalent to the risk of weighted assets, as denoted by the Tier I capital for banks.

The second is the CRR cost. Banks have to maintain cash with the RBI, which earns them nothing. There is an opportunity cost for this. The banks have to consider the cash deposits they need to keep with the RBI. This is computed as: Required CRR × [Marginal Cost ÷ (1 - CRR)].

The third is the tenor premium. The tenor is the balance period of the loan. The higher the duration of the loan, the higher will be the risk. To cover the risk, the bank charges a premium. By the way, a tenor premium is uniform across all loan types.

Finally, there are operating costs, which are associated with providing the loan, raising funds and running the daily operations. This is expressed as a percentage of capital.

Thus, you have the cost of marginal money, the CRR, tenor premium and OpEx.

Every month, the RBI asks banks to publish the MCLR for overnight, one-month, three-month, six-month and one-year maturities. Loans are given out as MCLR plus spread, which is the extra percentage the bank charges riskier accounts. Each month, as the MCLR changes, the interest on floating rate loans changes. Of course, the interest rate on fixed-rate loans does not change.

From 1 October 2019, the RBI allowed banks to use other benchmark rates instead of MCLR for home loans, business loans, working capital loans, etc. With this, banks can now offer external benchmark-linked loans connected to the RBI repo rate, Government of India treasury bills, etc.

In 2020, the RBI introduced long term repo operations for one- or two-year periods. The idea is to push banks to borrow at these lower rates and then in turn lend to NBFCs.

By the way, India follows the Basel Norms, which are aimed at coordinating banking regulations around the world. The norms have three aims: make banks strong enough to withstand financial stress, reduce risk in the system and improve transparency in functioning.

7

KRISHNA REVISES HIS NOTES

That night, sitting late, Krishna went through his notes. He wanted to condense them into a short write-up that he could put out in *Focus*, his school magazine. He wasn't sure if his economics teacher, who was the editor of the magazine, would approve of it, but he decided to give it a try nevertheless.

He began to write.

The recent collapse of the NBH is not the first such fall in India's long banking tradition. History is replete with these stories **(Note to self: I must add a few names after sounding out GGP).** In 1969, Mrs Indira Gandhi brought banks under government control by nationalizing them. Many believed it was a political masterstroke. Early on, there were several economic gains. Yet, in retrospect, nationalization sowed the seeds for the rot that came to be associated with banking.

Banks borrow money at a lower rate and lend it at a higher rate. The RBI is the regulator responsible for ensuring banks work responsibly. To provide liquidity so that there is no run, the RBI requires banks to maintain SLR and CRR, which at times is 25 per cent. This means only 75 per cent of the money raised is available for lending.

Banks collapse because they overextend their balance sheets by lending without caution. You can find if a bank is on a sticky wicket by looking at their CRAR. Anything less than 10 per cent is considered an early warning signal.

There are two types of assets: performing and non-performing. The former are also called standard assets, while the latter are abbreviated as NPA. Based on the period for which they are due within the NPA, they are classified as substandard, doubtful and loss assets. Based on such classification, income is recognized and provisions are made.

Leverage or borrowing is both an advantage and a disadvantage. The twin balance sheet crisis was a product of 'over-borrowing and over-lending, of unmitigated optimism in the India growth story', and a flawed economic model. Both corporates' and the banks' balance sheet had holes. It became a triple balance sheet problem when the NBFCs, to whom banks turned, fell by the wayside and became a full-blown four balance sheet crisis when infrastructure companies, to whom the NBFCs advanced money, collapsed.

He ended by putting down in bold red colours a note for himself: **In our subsequent sittings with GGP, Junior and I should ask him about the scandals that rocked the banking sector. I must also clarify with him the story of a mysterious aunt of mine.**

PART TWO

SCAMMING THE BANK

8

MUNDHRA AND NAGARWALA: CONMEN

Lobin Stephen Senior's two great-grandsons, Lobin Stephen Junior and Krishna McKenzie, were seated at the dinner table in their tastefully done living room. Senior's daughter, Larissa Iqbal, had joined them too. Senior was present too.

'What was post-Independence India's first financial scam?' asked Krishna, turning his attention to Larissa.

'Well, it was in 1957 when a Kolkata-based businessman, Haridas Mundhra convinced the Life Insurance Corporation, LIC, to invest ₹124 lakh in shares of six sinking companies in which he had interest. Mundhra was a rogue trader who had in the previous year been indicted for selling forged shares.' Larissa had once been a forensic auditor with the corporation (LIC).

Krishna was scribbling furiously. 'And do you by any chance remember what the six companies Mundhra was interested in?'

'Of course,' said his grand-aunt as she rattled off the names. 'Richardson & Cruddas Ltd, Jessop and Co., Smith Stanistreet, F. & C. Osler (India) Ltd, Agnelo Brothers and British India Corporation,' she paused and then added. 'Later investigations revealed that the investment was made under intense political pressure and without consulting the LIC's investment committee.'

After a 10-second silence, Senior announced, 'The LIC lost most of the money.'

Krishna whistled. 'The *LIC* lost money?' he asked incredulously. 'How long has the LIC been in business?'

Larissa knew this was Krishna's way of playing innocent. Of

course, he knew that the LIC was established in 1956. After all, Krishna was a star quizzer.

But she still went ahead to explain. '1956. Incidentally, it was Feroze Gandhi's initiatives that led to the formation of the LIC, when 245 firms were nationalized and consolidated into one corporation. Feroze was former prime minister Jawaharlal Nehru's son-in-law.'

Senior stepped in. 'In a reflection of how politics worked in those times, it was Feroze, himself a Congressman, who flagged the Mundhra scandal. He charged the then finance minister T.T. Krishnamachari and the then finance secretary H.M. Patel of crossing the line in pushing for the LIC's investment in those six companies.'

'So, what did Nehru do? Brush it under the carpet?' Junior asked.

'Far from it. In fact, Panditji appointed former Chief Justice of the Bombay High Court M.C. Chagla to inquire into the matter.

'Chagla worked with the speed of a cheetah and completed the report in 24 days. The hearings were conducted in public. Leading stockbrokers testified that the investment could not have been made for propping up the market, as was claimed by the finance ministry. After Chagla filed his report, Krishnamachari resigned and Mundhra was jailed for 22 years.

'Chagla held that the finance secretary, along with two LIC officials, may have colluded on the payment, but a subsequent inquiry by Justice Vivian Bose cleared their names. Justice Bose passed strictures against the finance minister for "lying".'

And then from her iPad, Larissa read out:

The Chagla Commission held that the market transaction was opposed to propriety. The Commission did not accept Patel's view that the Corporation had to buy the shares because many Mundhra shares would be sold at distressed prices, creating panic in the stock market. The Commission suggested that the LIC did the transaction on the government's order and that T.T. Krishnamachari had approved it. Parliament disagreed with this finding.

Junior summarized it. 'So, you are saying the finance minister and his secretary helped Mundhra by pushing the LIC to make equity purchases bypassing the LIC's investment committee, and that as a result, the corporation lost money as the share price collapsed. And there was an unsubstantiated charge that money changed hands between Mundhra and the Congress.'

'Substantially right,' said his grandmother. 'Shortly, I will mail you GGP's Eight Points that he had made note of in the 1960s. Do read it,' saying so she stepped out of the dining room to offer her last namaaz of the day. She had married outside her religion.

Junior remarked, 'So, the Mundhra scandal exposed the nexus among politicians, bureaucracy, stock market speculators and rogue businessmen.'

'Yup,' said Krishna. 'GGP promised that tomorrow he will tell us the story of Rustom Sohrab "Jimmy" Nagarwala.'

That night, an anxious Krishna sat in his bed. Sleep eluded him, as he was itching to hear about Nagarwala. He guessed that this case, too, might involve the Nehru-Gandhi family.

◆

The following morning, Krishna was raring to go. The previous night, he had gobbled the entire notes prepared by his GGP that his grand-aunt had shared with them.

'I want to hear more such stories,' he told no one in particular at the breakfast table.

His grand-aunt smiled. 'Do you want to listen to one involving Mrs Gandhi?'

'The Iron Lady? Why not.' His eyes danced with excitement. 'You mean the Jimmy Nagarwala case involved Mrs Gandhi?'

A small dimple formed on Larissa's cheek. At 65, she still sat ramrod straight and her beauty was intact.

'On 21 May 1971, a telephonic call came to Ved Prakash Malhotra, the head cashier at Parliament House Branch of the State Bank. The caller identified himself as P.N. Haksar, principal secretary to the prime minister. He asked the banker to hold on the line as he connected to Mrs Gandhi.'

'And then what happened?' asked Krishna.

'Malhotra, a person will approach you using the code: *Bangladesh ka Babu*. You should say *Bar-at-law* and deliver ₹60 lakh.'

This was not Larissa's voice, it was her imitating someone else. Taken aback, the quiz buff asked, 'Are you mimicking Mrs Gandhi? Why?'

'Yes, because that is what the caller did. They sounded exactly like the Prime Minister, so Malhotra rushed to implement the instructions.' Larissa paused for a moment and continued. 'Two guards loaded the cash trunk into the car, which was driven away by Malhotra. He delivered the money to Nagarwala, but when he went to the PMO to get a receipt, Haksar told him there was no such instruction to pay.

'Hereabout, multiple views are given about the events. One view is that Malhotra's deputy was concerned by his boss's long absence of more than a couple of hours, so called in the cops, and after that it was difficult to cover the track. Another view is that Haksar asked the head cashier to inform the police. Whichever it was, the police took up the investigation. Within 24 hours, Nagarwala was found, arrested and most of the money recovered. Five days later, on 26 May, Nagarwala confessed to impersonation and theft, was convicted in a 10-minute court trial and sentenced to four years of imprisonment.'

'Uff!' said Krishna. 'What was Nagarwala's explanation?'

'In his confession, Nagarwala said he dreamed up the scheme at the spur of the moment to draw attention to the Bangladesh crisis. He was convicted based on his confession.'

Junior chipped in. 'But where was the circumstantial evidence to back what he said?'

'None. There was a suggestion that Nagarwala was an undercover agent working for India to support guerillas in Bangladesh and that the government was washing its hands off the case after the police got involved,' said Larissa.

Krishna was incredulous. 'Just like that?'

'Some days later, Nagarwala filed an appeal for retrial, but his plea was rejected. On 16 November, Nagarwala said his case should not be proceeded with until the investigation against Malhotra was completed. Four days later, the young police officer D.K. Kashyap, who had headed the investigation, was killed in a car accident while going for his honeymoon.

'Nagarwala sent a message to D.F. Karaka, the editor of *Current*, saying he would like to give him an interview. However, as the editor was ill, his assistant came in his place, but Nagarwala refused to entertain the latter.

'A few weeks passed, and on 2 March 1972, Nagarwala had a cardiac arrest while in prison. It was his fifth-first birthday.'

'OMG!' exclaimed Krishna, surprised at the sudden turn of events. 'This is like a murder mystery! What is the truth?'

Larissa explained, 'Here is one possible sequence of events that may have taken place. In May 1971, the government had come to realize that a war with Pakistan was inevitable. Camps to train volunteers had been set up and they needed money to buy ammunition. Nagarwala, who was an ex-military intelligence officer in the British army, had been coordinating with the Bangladesh intelligence. He had been authorized to collect the amount and fly to Kolkata. The urgency of the demand necessitated telephonic orders. Malhotra was the only officer entitled to handle secret funds. He knew Nagarwala from before.

'What happened was that when Malhotra went to collect the voucher, the deputy chief cashier, worried over his boss's disappearance for over 90 minutes, lodged a complaint. The news spread like wildfire, and it was too late to hush up the case.'

Krishna wondered aloud, 'So, the case died there?'

'Actually, far from it. In 1978, the Janata Party government, the first non-Congress central government since Independence, established an inquiry commission under Justice P. Jaganmohan Reddy, which later issued an 800-page report that raised more questions than it offered answers. It reported that the bank had kept unaccounted assets and the PMO did not co-operate with the investigation. It held that the confession should have been rejected as it lacked evidence.'

'So was Nagarwala killed?' asked Krishna.

'The committee found that there was no reason to suspect foul play in Nagarwala's death,' said Larissa, standing up.

Krishna groaned, 'That's an unsatisfying end.'

His cousin Junior agreed with him.

In his notepad, Krishna scribbled: 'Mundhra was a crook. About Nagarwala, I don't know. But in either case, the Congress party is not coming out smelling of roses.'

THE MUNDHRA SCANDAL

(Based on newspaper reports of those times)

1. The government treated the LIC as an internal department instead of allowing it to work freely.

2. LIC's investments in Mundhra companies were examined by (a) the Chagla Commission, (b) the Vivian Bose Board of Inquiry, and (c) the Union Public Service Commission. Each came with differing views.

3. The Chagla Commission held that H.M. Patel was wrong in believing that the LIC needed to invest in Mundhra shares to stave off a payment crisis in the Calcutta market. It further held that the government ordered, not advised, the Corporation to make those investments and T.T. Krishnamachari toed with Patel and approved the transaction.

4. The Vivian Bose Board found Patel guilty of abusing his authority in asking two officers to do the transaction and was negligent since he did not indicate the prices at which they were to be bought. It held that Patel's act was not covered by ministerial approval.

5. The Union Public Service Commission held that Patel did not abuse his authority and that he was not negligent. Instead, it held Kamat, the chairman of LIC, negligent. It concluded that Krishnamachari was aware of the antecedents of Mundhra.

6. The government dropped the charges against Patel, and imposed the penalty of censure on Kamat.

7. The Vivian Board felt that the investment was a quid pro quo for a donation to the Congress party. But the charge could not be sustained.

8. Clearly, the autonomy of the Corporation was compromised within a year of its birth and this did not augur well for a new nation.

9

HARSHAD MEHTA: THE PIED PIPER

'Ma-Ma, where were you when the Harshad Mehta case happened?' asked Junior, addressing Larissa.

'Well, that was in 1992. I had just graduated from St Stephen's and received a call from the Indian Institute of Management, Calcutta, IIM-C.'

'What was it like?' said Junior.

'India had just lost Rajiv Gandhi, its most charismatic politician. When he first assumed office, we knew Rajiv was addressing our generation with his promise to take India into the twenty-first century. Those were Camelot days, and he was King Arthur.'

'You seem to be in love with the man who became a byword in corruption?' said Junior.

'That's unfair! There was no proof of a payoff. Incidentally, the Bofors gun did a marvelous job in the Kargil War. But in a way, you are right: my generation loved him. After all, he was our first yuppie politician, westernized in his outlook and a breath of fresh air in the murky world of politics. And yes, Bofors haunted the Gandhis, an election was lost on its cause and the stigma stuck forever.'

'So, what happened?'

'Okay, the Congress formed a minority government under a retired politician who dragged in a semi-retired bureaucrat to be his finance minister. Prime Minister Narasimha Rao and Dr Manmohan Singh worked magic as India walked the road of becoming a market economy. If my generation as well as yours have seen prosperity, we have them to thank.'

'That's fine. I was asking about Mehta?' said Junior.

'Ha. Mehta. The Big Bull.'

'Ma-Ma, you are mixing up names. Rakesh Jhunjhunwala was the big bull,' corrected Krishna.

She smiled. 'The original big bull was Harshad Mehta. When Dr Singh opened up the economy, the market raced ahead, and as later events showed, Mehta had a key role to play in this growth. Alas, it turned out to be the role of a rogue trader.'

'I read the article GGP had distributed last year. There were a few terms that I really didn't understand. Can you explain them?'

'Sure, go ahead. You can ask me.'

'What is replacement cost theory?'

'It is actually old hat but became very popular after Mehta used it to explain his purchase of Associated Cement Company (ACC) stock. He said that shares of a manufacturing company should be valued at what it would cost today to set up a similar plant.'

'Interesting! But why did you call it old hat?' asked Junior.

'Long ago, in 1956, in the Lok Sabha, a Member of Parliament, P.D. Himatsingka, explained the stock price rise of IISCO through this theory. He had said that if IISCO, set up at an initial cost of ₹5.2 crore, rose in stock price from ₹10 to ₹36, the cost of setting up a new steel plant had increased 20 times to ₹100 crore. It meant the stock price had only increased about threefold, whereas the cost of the plant had increased twentyfold. And that if someone took a 100 per cent stake in IISCO, it would cost him only about ₹19 crore (₹5.2 crore x 3.6 times) and that this was dirt cheap.'

'Something like Tobin's Q?' asked Junior.

Krishna stared. 'Don't show off.'

Larissa concealed her smile. 'Yeah.' And then turning towards Krishna, she said, 'Tobin's Q is the ratio between a physical asset's market value and its replacement value. It was first conceptualized by Nicholas Kaldor in 1966 and popularized by James Tobin in the 1970s.'

'So, if Tobin's Q is less than 1, it means the asset is undervalued?' asked Krishna, showing remarkable grasp of the topic.

'Sort of,' said Junior, in grudging admiration.

Krishna said, 'I read GGP's note, and it was all Greek and Latin to me. What are these ready-forward transactions that Mehta dealt in?'

Larissa said, 'In simple terms, it means simultaneous purchase and sale. For instance, I have an Infosys share. I am selling it to you today at ₹1,700 and agree to repurchase it 15 days later at ₹1,725. I would do that if I want to borrow money. I buy back at a higher price because the difference is the interest you want for having lent money to me. The ₹25 on ₹1,700 for 15 days is the equivalent of 36 per cent per annum.'

'So, it is indirectly lending money against a security?' asked Krishna.

'Yes, absolutely.'

'And what is banker's receipt?' asked Krishna.

'The securities typically don't change hands. In our example, I don't hand over the Infosys share, as it will come back to me in any case. In trust, a receipt is scribbled out, which is called the banker's receipt,' answered Larissa.

Junior said, 'The funny thing is that the receipt itself got traded.'

Krishna was puzzled. 'Wait, what?'

'Go read the write-up a couple of more times. You will get a finer understanding of it, Brat,' Junior teased.

'Well, I have understood most of it. What I am not able to understand is, how did the bankers let it happen?'

Larissa said, 'Well, everyone has a lever which, when triggered, can make them do what you want them to do. Harshad Mehta found the trigger in the greedy bankers.'

Saying so, Larissa got up to tell them that she would be flying out to Singapore for work.

Krishna would not let her go. 'Don't tell me these scandals happened only in India.'

'Well, not exactly. Crowd psychology is rooted in history. Many stories are captured in Charles Mackay's book *Extraordinary Popular Delusions and the Madness of Crowds.*' Turning to Junior, she said, 'You must read that book.'

Hurt, Krishna asked, 'Do you mean I won't understand it?'

'*Harry Potter* suits you best,' taunted Junior.

Larissa promised the boys she would leave a note on two stories—the 'Mississippi Company' and 'Tulip mania'.

'I intend to read the chapter "Popular Admiration for Great Thieves",' said Krishna.

Larissa stared. 'What? How do you know that?'

'Brat googles faster than he thinks!' Junior teased his cousin.

THE BIG BULL

Harshad Mehta was the first superstar of the Indian stock market.

Of course, before him, there was Dhirubhai Ambani, but while the former petrol pump attendant generously rewarded his shareholders, Mehta played the role of the Pied Piper to perfection. He seduced middle-class India, which had just begun to explore the market economy.

It was remarkable that this one man, once a clerk in an insurance company, fooled the entire country's banking system that is supposed to house men of great intellect. And despite playing the master manipulator in what was unarguably the biggest scandal of its time, Mehta will be remembered more as a cult hero than a sleazy villain.

Born in 1954 in a Gujarati Jain family of modest means, Mehta didn't set the Ganges on fire either in school or college. He had come to Mumbai, the City of Dreams, to make a mark. After a series of flop shows at work, he joined a stockbroker, from whom he learnt the tools of the trade.

A few years later, Mehta established his own brokering house, and by early 1990, came to be popularly known as the 'Big Bull'. The media went gaga over him, focussing on his flashy lifestyle, 15,000-square-feet penthouse and a fleet of cars. He was known for his keen eye for undervalued stocks, and once they were identified by him and bought, they would rise.

When he propounded his famed replacement cost theory, even the high and mighty began to eat out of his hand. He argued that the stock of a manufacturing company should be valued at what it would cost to set up a similar plant. This theory found many takers, and interestingly, it sent ACC from ₹200 to ₹9,000 even as Mehta linked the rise to this argument of his.

Soon, he would be 'teeming and lading' and 'pumping the market' with the help of fake bank receipts, which his firm exchanged for ready-forward transactions between banks, and bring the banking system to its knees. Teeming and lading is a method by which a person who takes payments uses the money personally for some days and posts the transaction later. A common practice here is that the amounts received from a subsequent debtor is credited to the earlier debtor's account so that one debtor's account does not show an outstanding balance for a long time. Such a process is continued until the time the original amount misappropriated is finally replaced.

Pump-and-dump is a manipulative scheme to boost the price of a stock through fake recommendations.

Background to the Fraud

In 1991, Dr Manmohan Singh opened up the Indian economy, dusting off the cobwebs of socialism. This brought an animal spirit to the market, and an intense competition in business. The banking sector hadn't yet been opened to private players, but there still was pressure on them to report profits.

In those days, banks in India were not allowed to invest in the equity market, but they had to maintain SLR and CRR, which help determine the liquidity in the banking system. While the former is the cash balance that banks must keep with the RBI, the latter is a reserve that commercial banks must maintain in the form of approved securities. Both are a percentage of the bank's net demand and time liabilities.

As the return from CRR was nil, and that on SLR was less than the cost of capital, it would push the rate at which banks would lend, as less money was now available. Add to that the fact that banks were mandated to give loans to the priority sector; there was an understandable pressure on the bottom line. Therefore, in order to ramp up profits, banks found ways and means to beat the system.

Harshad Mehta understood the system inside out.

The sweet-talking broker promised the bank higher interest rates while asking them to transfer money into his personal account to buy government securities from other banks. Mehta used this money lying in his account not to buy the promised government securities, but to buy more and more shares. It caused the stock prices to skyrocket. He would then sell them and pass off a part of the proceeds to the bank's pocket. No one was any wiser.

An attendant transaction to this was the ready-forward transaction involving two banks and a broker. In this deal, the broker's job is to bring the banks together for a fee. His role is supposed to end there, and he is not supposed to handle either the cash or the security, although that is not how it panned out. What happened was the seller gave the security to the broker for onward transmission to the buyer, and the buyer made the payment to the broker for onward settlement with the seller. So, the money sat with the broker for some time.

Also, in such transactions, securities do not move up and down. Instead, the seller and buyer exchange a banker's receipt, which is issued by the seller and confirms that he has the securities and has carried out the transaction. Since brokers brokered the deals, the banker's receipt was handed over to the broker for onward transmission. Mehta now passed them on to buying banks, which gave Mehta money to pay the first bank.

Mehta pumped the money into the equity market. In those days, settlement of transactions had a lead time of 15 days, while trades on Indian stock exchanges were settled within two days after they take place, known as T+2 (trade date plus two days) settlement. The shares were sold at a profit, and the amount outstanding to the bank was settled.

The game went on as long as stock prices hit the stratosphere, but once the fraud was exposed, banks were left holding worthless, fake banker's receipts in the name of securities and had been swindled off by an estimated ₹4,025 crore in 1991 terms. At an average inflation rate of 7.15 per cent, this translates to ₹34,239 crore in 2022 terms.

Trust, but Verify

There is another angle to this. When banks face temporary surges in their deposits, they have to increase their bond holdings. As it would be cumbersome to go through the whole process of buying bonds, they were authorized by the law to lend and borrow these securities through ready-forward transaction, which is effectively a 15-day loan from one bank to another and is backed by government bonds as security.

However, instead of transferring the bonds, the bank would issue a banker's receipt, because while the bond certificates would be worth say ₹100 crore, the bank's SLR requirements would be far lower. This is akin to giving a ₹100 note to buy a ₹15 bus ticket, and the conductor scribbles on the back of your ticket that he owes you ₹85. This note for ₹85 is similar to a banker's receipt.

After 15 days, the borrowing bank would buy back the banker's receipt at a higher price, the difference being the interest. Because of banker's receipts, there would be no actual transfer of securities, and instead, the banker's receipts would be simply canceled and returned.

In all this, brokers should act merely as middlemen who bring two parties together for a fee. Instead, they also served as conduits to receive certificates, make payments and route the money through their personal accounts. In the small window of time available for the repayment, Mehta, the 'honest middleman', pumped the money into the equity market. It was the old-fashioned teeming-and-lading that one reads about as part of 'Auditing 101' in colleges.

Why Did Banks Trade in Securities?

As already indicated, the RBI mandates banks to maintain a CRR and an SLR as part of prudent banking. During those days, the former earned no interest, and for the latter, banks earned a small return.

When the RBI increased CRR, some banks would be short of cash, and when they upped the SLR, some banks would be short of securities. This created a market for securities. Of course, the banks could have borrowed from the call money market. Call money is a short-term money payable when called out to pay. Unlike a term loan, which has a defined maturity, call money does not have a fixed schedule. Whenever the lender wishes, they can ask back the money. However, banks were not willing to lend in the call market because in the late 1980s, the interest rate was frozen at 10 per cent. They were okay with the ready-forward transaction because they could lend even at above 10 per cent!

According to the law, banker's receipts could be issued only for public sector undertaking (PSU) bonds or mutual fund units and not for government securities. Also, banker's receipts were valid for 90 days only. The record of government securities was required to be maintained in the RBI's subsidiary general ledger (SGL). Transfers were to be effected only through an SGL transfer form presented to the RBI for making entries.

The banks, however, issued banker's receipts even for transactions in government securities and would not insist on delivery within the 90-day limit. If the securities didn't change hands in the agreed time, they would sell those securities to a third bank and issue another banker's receipt. So, banker's receipts were issued with banker's receipts as the underlying! With banker's receipts clandestinely substituting transfer forms, the SGL would be at variance in reality.

Why Were Banks Willing to Accommodate Brokers?

Brokers helped banks meet statutory stipulations and also earn profits on their securities transactions. In addition, they temporarily bore the bank's losses. For example, when the RBI hikes interest rates, the value of the bonds held by banks would decline, in line with bond valuation theory. The banks would park some of the loss-making bonds with brokers to reduce the hit on their earnings. The brokers would absorb losses on some transactions and get in other trades.

Mehta stepped up the ante with a couple of banks, such as the Bank of Karad and the Metropolitan Cooperative Bank. He even created fake banker's receipts and passed them on to buying banks. These banks gave money to Mehta, thinking they were lending against government securities while actually lending against thin air. An RBI audit would later show that the value of banker's receipts in circulation far exceeded the government bonds held by the banks.

How Did the Cat Finally Get out of the Bag?

In January 1992, the RBI's inspectors found irregularities in banks' securities transactions. In April, they discovered that there were no securities for ₹649 crore, which the SBI had paid Mehta. When the SBI called for return of the money, Mehta coughed up ₹620 crore. When the auditors dug deeper, they found that he produced this from his Grindlays Bank account. There was nothing wrong with that, except that the National Housing Bank (NHB) cheques drawn in favour of Grindlays Bank and credited to Mehta's account funded a good part of it. As later events revealed, it was a securities transaction between the NHB and Grindlays, and the former did not have any securities to show for it. The cat was finally out of the bag.[23]

The Janakiraman Committee was subsequently set up to investigate the fraud. It narrowed down to the exposure of seven financial

---

[23]Nair, Santosh, 'Scam 1992 Explained: How Harshad Mehta, Brokers and Banks Gamed the System', CNBC TV 18, 25 March 2022, https://bit.ly/3W7UjQV. Accessed on 12 December 2022.

institutions: Andhra Bank Financial Services, Canbank Financial Services, Canbank Mutual Fund, NHB, State Bank of Saurashtra, SBI Capital Markets and Standard Chartered Bank. The committee found that these seven entities had in all forked out a whopping ₹4,024 crore to other institutions for government securities and PSU bonds without having the securities to show for the money paid![24]

Meanwhile, the market capitalization tanked by ₹100,000 crore.

The cops arrested Harshad Mehta, the soft-spoken man who had been the darling of Dalal Street. Former CBI officer K. Madhavan, the safari-clad super-sleuth who handled the Bofors scandal earlier and aced international cricket's match-fixing scandal later, was asked to head the investigation against Mehta.

Meanwhile, on 16 June 1993, the Big Bull claimed that he handed over a suitcase with ₹1 crore cash to Prime Minister Rao as bribe. When the media wondered if so much money could be packed into a box, he demonstrated how ₹67 lakh could get there. No one bought the explanation, as it was unimaginable that any party would take a bribe of just a crore! The CBI never found any evidence to substantiate Mehta's charge.

Foreign banks did not emerge smelling of roses out of Madhavan's investigation. There were irregularities in the portfolio management services (PMS) operations. Citibank short-sold government securities, which meant that it sold securities it did not own, in gross violation of RBI's rules. The Joint Parliamentary Committee (JPC) report named ANZ Grindlays, American Express Bank, Bank of America, Citibank and Standard Chartered as significant players who set off the chain of events that led to the scam.[25] They were spared any serious consequences because India was then in a fragile foreign exchange situation. We had to depend on loans and credits from foreign banks.

The PSUs, too, had been trapped in a crisis of their own making. When the government withdrew budgetary support, they began raising

[24]Ibid.
[25]Ibid.

money in the bond market. When there were not enough takers, a deal was struck with banks under which the banks would subscribe, and in return, the PSUs placed the funds in the banks' PMS.

In September 1999, the Bombay High Court convicted Mehta and sentenced him to five years of imprisonment. The Supreme Court upheld this judgment. His legal battles continued until 2001, when he suffered a cardiac arrest while in jail. It was 31 December and he was 47 years of age. The man had gone too soon, leaving a terrible legacy that's hard to forget. Maybe if he had lived and the government had the foresight, he could have worked for the government in later years, as an investigator, the way Federal Bureau of Investigation used Frank Abagnale!

Nearly 21 years after Harshad Mehta's death, his wife Jyoti claimed that his death happened because jail staff withheld medical care for four hours. She asserted that her family had won more than 1,200 substantial litigations launched against them in judicial forums.

MISSISSIPPI COMPANY

In France, when King Louis XIV died in 1715, the country was almost bankrupt. At that point, economist John Law presented a revival plan to Philippe I, Duke of Orleans, the younger son of Louis XIII.

Law convinced the Duke to establish a state-owned bank to receive gold in place of paper currency, promising that the paper could be redeemed for gold on demand. He told the Duke that the State must lend cash to entrepreneurs, collect interest from the loan and pay off the national debt.

Next, Law created the Mississippi Company. It was given the exclusive right to trade with Louisiana in the US. America was a growing economy, and the prospect of making it big in Mississippi excited people. Soon, investors exchanged their debt investment for shares in this company. The stock prices hit new highs. Whenever it fell, Law printed more fiat money (paper currency) to pump the prices. What the investors didn't know was that Louisiana was a swamp, and there was no way that it would lead to riches.

When people realized the bank was giving out more receipts than gold in the system, a run on the bank started. People began selling Mississippi shares; it became worthless overnight, and many fortunes were lost as a result.

The Mississippi bubble was an early version of the get-rich-quick schemes that we see today. Here, the government was indirectly a party to the fraud.

TULIP MANIA

Almost a hundred years before the Mississippi case, another case of inflated prices occurred in Holland, which has always been known for its gorgeous tulips.

In 1637, the tulip prices touched an incredible peak—a tulip bulb sold for 10 times the annual income of an artisan. At another time, 12 acres of land were offered for a single bulb.

The price led to ridiculous situations—a sailor was arrested when he was found eating a tulip bulb. The poor man had mistaken the tulip bulb for an onion. The cost of his breakfast might have regaled a whole ship's crew for a year!

In 1636, a futures market emerged for trading in bulbs. The price of tulips skyrocketed due to rampant speculation. People were buying for fear of missing out. They hoped to resell at a huge profit. Some contracts changed hands 10 times in a day. Such a market was too good to last.

In February 1637, buyers simply vanished. Once this realization set in, the demand for tulips collapsed, and the bubble burst.

10

KETAN PAREKH: THE BOMBAY BULL

Lobin Stephen Senior got up at the crack of dawn. He made himself a cup of tea and then went out for his morning walk. Giving him company was his daughter Larissa.

Larissa was anxious about her grandson with whom she often had conflicts, as with every teenager. 'Dad, I have seen you talking to Junior a lot recently. How is he shaping up?' she asked, her voice laced with worry.

'He is good. Otherwise, he would not have got into Harvard.'

'I know. But I just wanted your view. After all, Harvard is a competitive place, and I am concerned if he will get top grades.'

'He is fine, in fact, remarkable, but I am more excited about Krishna. He is so quick on the uptake, and for a boy his age, he is exceptionally sharp.'

A smile crossed Larissa's face. 'Is it?'

The McKenzies had died in a car accident, and that had caused Larissa temporary depression. But getting custody of Krishna brought her sanity back. The tragedy happened five years ago, but it was like yesterday.

Senior continued to walk. 'Larissa, this morning, over breakfast, I am meeting the two boys to discuss the Ketan Parekh scam. You, too, join in to see how they are growing.'

'Oh, that won't be possible, unfortunately. I have some work to finish. In any case, we discussed the Harshad Mehta scandal when you were away.'

'Okay, that's good. But you're always welcome.'

'Hmm… Well, on second thought, I will join you.'

◆

Senior, Junior and Krishna were at the table, and the resident cook was serving them masala dosas.

'So, did you two read up on KP?' asked Senior.

'Yes, I did early this morning. Last night, I had to complete some assignments for college,' said Junior.

'GGP, I read it once, then I reread it. You really have a very engaging way of writing. Never knew that.' It was Krishna.

Senior's eyes lit up. What Krishna didn't know was that long before making it into banking, Senior was a journalist of some consequence.

'I am sure you understood nothing in the write-up, Brat,' teased Junior.

'On the contrary, I understood most of it,' retorted Krishna.

'Okay, tell me what it was about?' said Junior.

'So, Ketan Parekh used "pump-and-dump" to ramp up the stock price of his K-10 portfolio and then sold it at a profit. He did circuit trading to inject artificial life into the stocks and got money by bribing bankers.'

'Not bad. Not bad at all. How long did it take you to mug up these sentences?' teased Junior.

Krishna was a cramming machine, but he ignored the jibe. 'GGP, honestly, what exactly is "pump-and-dump"? I know it is jacking up the price of a stock through misleading reports and then selling it at a higher price. Once operators "dump", as in sell the overvalued shares, the price falls and investors lose money. But how is it executed?'

The cook had sliced Larissa's and Senior's dosa into three parts. Larissa used her knife to cut off a small piece of it. She dipped one into a small bowl of sambhaar, picked it up with a fork and gingerly placed it in the inner recess of her mouth.

'Krishna, let me give you an example.' She was the only one who never called him Brat. 'Suppose I had 10,000 shares of a company that I bought at ₹12. This stock is thinly traded. I now tell you and nine others that a top mutual fund manager has said to me that this share will touch ₹72 in a year. What will you do?'

'I will ask you if you have bought the shares.'

Senior grinned, turning towards Larissa, and raised his eyebrows, suggesting *I told you so*!

'Well said,' remarked Larissa, nodding. 'I will tell each of you that I have bought 10,000 shares. So, now the 10 of you will buy 10,000 shares each, and suddenly the stock has traded a volume of 100,000. This itself can push the price up to ₹12.50.'

'Demand and supply,' chipped in Junior.

'You will now mentally multiply 10,000 shares with the profit of ₹0.5 and be happy with the ₹5,000. What will you do next?' asked Larissa.

The very thought of making a profit excited Krishna. 'I will tell 10 of my friends what you told me, and I will tell them I have made a profit ₹5,000.'

'Excellent! So will the 10 people you had spoken to. Each of you has now pushed 10 more to buy, which means 100 people are suddenly buying in all 10,000 x 100 = 1,000,000 shares. This will pump up the price to say ₹14.5.'

Krishna was thrilled. 'So, those 100 people will tell 10 each, and we will have 1,000 people buying 10,000 shares or a volume of ₹100 lakh.'

'Yes. As people see the volume go up, more folks will join the party. That will take the stock price into the stratosphere, past the upper circuit multiple times. Soon, the stock will touch, say, ₹60, and now maybe the volume of shares being traded is 60 crore.'

'What happens next?' asked Krishna, in anticipation, then gave the answer himself. 'At this point, you, Ma-Ma, will sell your 10,000 shares and tell the 10 of us that you are selling. We will tell the 10 others to whom we had sounded to sell. Suddenly, a selling wave takes place, which leads to panic selling, and the stock returns to where it belonged—₹12. Right?'

'Bang on,' said Larissa, and Krishna whistled silently. 'I would have made a profit of ₹480,000 ([60-12] x 10,000 = ₹480,000).'

During this discussion, Krishna had only taken one bite of the dosa. Now he attacked it like any hungry boy would. No knife and no fork for him. He used his hand. And said, 'Wait, I have one more question.'

The family discussed other things and allowed Krishna to have his half-dozen dosas.

A while later, with his stomach full, Krishna asked, '*Yeh circular trading kya hai?* (What is this circular trading?).' Nobody knew why he suddenly broke into Hindi. Sometimes he just liked showing off.

Senior explained, 'In the pump-and-dump example, we discussed 1,000-odd people buying shares. But often, it is difficult to reach out to so many people. So, what KP did was to assemble a group of friends, and they constantly bought and sold between themselves. Like you sell 1,000 to Junior, and in the next 30 minutes, he sells 1,000 to you, and this ding-dong continues all through the day. This pushes up the "traded volumes". The investors who base their decisions on the volume traded will consider such stocks to be active and invest in them. This, in turn, leads to a price rise, and at an appropriate time, the manipulator exits.'

'Sounds interesting!' said Junior and Krishna in chorus.

The tea had come, and it was time for Senior to watch the news. 'If you have no more questions, reread my piece a couple of times more, now that you have understood the terms.'

KETAN'S K-10

Ketan Parekh, aka KP, a CA by training, was a stockbroker with the Midas touch. Whichever stock he traded in turned to gold. Unfortunately, instead of using his intelligence to become a Warren Buffett or George Soros, he became an economic offender.

Parekh began his career in the late 1980s running his father's family business named NH Securities, an institutional brokerage firm. There, he learnt the mechanics of market operations. At some point, he came in contact with Harshad Mehta and soon began working for him.

Later events show that he was a co-conspirator with the Big Bull. He was part of the Canbank Mutual Fund scam of 1992, in which the money received for buying government securities from them was diverted towards the accounts of stockbrokers.

KP's best years began in 1999. That was when dotcom was capturing the public imagination. He talked about the impending Information, Communication, and Entertainment revolution. The e-commerce movement had led to a huge rise in the value of technology stocks across the globe. Indian markets too, saw a secular rise.

Cult Status

When a few of KP's predictions came true, the man emerged as a cult figure. Market players, cinestars, corporate honchos and politicians broke bread with him. Several investment firms, banks, overseas corporates and businessmen asked him to manage their money. He even got Australian media tycoon Kerry Packer to co-promote KVP Ventures—a venture capital firm founded by KP that focussed on investing money in start-ups.

KP hand-picked 10 stocks and created a portfolio. These were: Pentamedia Graphics, HFCL, GTL, Silverline Technologies, Ranbaxy, Zee Telefilms, Global Trust Bank, DSQ Software, Aftek Infosys and SSI. Known as K-10 stocks, they had a small capital base and hence were low on liquidity. On them, he applied the 'pump-and-dump' formula.

Mutual funds like Alliance Capital, ICICI Prudential Fund and UTI also invested in K-10 stocks. Their net asset value rose vertically. By January 2000, K-10 stocks featured regularly amongst the top-five traded stocks.

Though KP lived in Mumbai, he used the Calcutta Stock Exchange (CSE) to trade because it lacked strict rules. He got several brokers to buy and sell on his behalf for a commission. At times, he colluded with promoters to ramp up stock prices. No one was any wiser. Once the stock prices went up, he would exit with a neat profit.

And unlike his mentor, Mehta, he would not make any noise about his exploits or flaunt his money in any way. He was soft-spoken and unassuming, but shrewd and ruthless.

The CSE was critical of KP's operation for two reasons. One, the regulation was lax, and this allowed volatile trade. And two, it helped him hide his operations from Mumbai brokers. Brokers at the CSE bought shares at KP's behest. KP would cover any losses that occurred due to a fall in stock price and pay a 2.5 per cent weekly interest to the brokers. His efforts coincided with the dotcom boom, and he was lauded for his ability to pick the right stock at the right time.

For instance, Pentafour Software stock prices zoomed from ₹175 to ₹2,700, while Global Telesystems rose from ₹185 to ₹3,100.[26] The price of Zee Telefilms shot up from ₹127 to ₹2,330, VisualSoft touched ₹8,448 from ₹625 in no time,[27] and Sonata Software rose from ₹90 to ₹2,936.[28] He pushed the price of HFCL from ₹42 to ₹2,300. He then used these high-paid stocks as collateral to get loans from banks.[29]

---

[26]Khanna, Sundeep, 'Backstory: Ketan Parekh and his K-10 stocks', CNBC TV 18, 20 September 2021, https://bit.ly/3Wi02o9. Accessed on 31 October 2022.

[27]Samaddar, Deb P., 'Ketan Parekh Scam: All That You Must Know', *Insider*, 16 March 2020, https://bit.ly/3OlpSUY. Accessed on 17 November 2022.

[28]'2001-Ketan Parekh Scam: Stock and Bull Story', *India Today*, 25 December 2005, https://bit.ly/3V60kgw. Accessed on 17 November 2022.

[29]Samaddar, Deb P., 'Ketan Parekh Scam: All That You Must Know', *Insider*, 16 March 2020, https://bit.ly/3OlpSUY. Accessed on 17 November 2022.

Bank Money

KP laid a trap on the Gujarat-based Madhavpura Mercantile Cooperative Bank (MMCB). As a first step, he bought its shares, and with that, approached them for a loan paid with pay orders. In 1999–2000, the bank started lending large sums of money to stockbrokers, including KP, violating the RBI's rules. It began by exceeding prescribed lending limits and later started loaning first and collecting collateral later, making it an unsecured loan in the intervening period. While the RBI allowed banks to give out loans to companies up to ₹15 crore, the officials allegedly took bribes to lend ₹800 crore without any collateral. These amounts of money were then paid through pay orders. KP promptly got these pay orders discounted at the Bank of India, meaning that, for example, he gave a pay order for ₹100 and collected ₹97.

When the market crashed in March 2001 and KP lost, there was a run on MMCB. Finally, in 2012, the RBI revoked the bank's licence after it could not repay public deposits.

Meanwhile, in March 2001, as the dotcom bubble burst, traders and brokers started dumping the K-10 stocks. KP, who had significant leveraged positions in these stocks, was now stuck.

A bear cartel started hammering the K-10 stocks, and KP was limping without cash.

One bright morning, KP liquidated his entire ownership of the K-10 stocks that he had bought and whose price he had pushed up over the past two years. He carried out this large-scale dump after trading hours, from five in the evening to midnight. This created a market crash the next day, and several large institutional investors lost their shirts. In Calcutta, it triggered a payment crisis, and investors lost close to ₹2,000 crore.

Following the 1 March crash, the Securities and Exchange Board of India (SEBI), the stock market regulator of India, decided to investigate the volatility of stock markets and inspect the books of brokers. Meanwhile, the RBI asked banks for data on their capital market exposure. This was based on a suspicion that the private player, Global Trust Bank, had exceeded the capital exposure norms and contributed to the market volatility.

The MMCB pay order issue hit several public sector banks. These included biggies like the SBI, Bank of India and PNB. There was also a charge that Global Trust Bank issued loans to KP far ahead of prescribed limits.

A 30-member Joint Parliamentary Committee investigation ensued, and it discovered that KP had rigged prices of Indian companies from 1995 up to 2001. It resulted in his first conviction, a one-year sentence for a 1992-transaction involving Canara Bank Mutual Fund.

The market crash pushed the much-needed modernization. The trading cycle was reduced from one week to one day. Operators were not allowed to carry forward trade. Exchange-traded derivatives were introduced. In a sense, KP forced lethargic policymakers to institute reforms in the financial system.

SEBI imposed restrictions on short sales and ordered that all sales must be backed by deliveries. It suspended the broker member directors of the Bombay Stock Exchange's governing board and banned trading by all stock exchange presidents, vice presidents and treasurers.

Eventually, KP was convicted and barred from trading till 2017. He was sentenced to rigorous imprisonment in March 2014, while the RBI cancelled MMCB's licence in 2012. Meanwhile, the Global Trust Bank had gone belly-up and merged with the Oriental Bank of Commerce in 2004. In May 2018, the Bank of India recovered the entire amount due from Parekh.

11

VIJAY MALLYA: GROUNDED

'Don't you think Vijay Mallya's hairstyle is quite interesting?' said Junior as Senior, Larissa, Krishna and he drove to the beach. Junior was at the wheel.

'More than his hair, you should be interested in the kind of money he made,' said Krishna. He looked out, watching the sun begin to kiss the sea at the horizon.

'Well, most of it was his dad's money, I guess, and the willful defaulter that the son was, he threw it all away,' said Junior.

'I think you just have a problem with people who earn a lot,' said the little one, sounding annoyed.

Larissa intervened diplomatically. 'Mallya may have a lot going against him, but he also had many things going in his favour.'

Junior understood where she was coming from and kept quiet. A few minutes later, as they stopped at a red light, he said, 'By the way, I understand he robbed 17 banks.'

'You can't say he "robbed" them. In a robbery, you take money behind people's backs without their consent. Here, he borrowed money for his business. It was not his fault his business failed. And if no one went behind the owners of failed businesses or those who ground their businesses to dust, why pick on Mallya?' Krishna was clearly a Mallya fan.

Looking into the rear mirror, Junior remarked, 'You are right in saying you cannot hold it against him if his business failed. By law, a company is a separate legal entity, distinct from the people who hold its shares. A shareholder cannot be asked to pay the company's debts.'

'Okay, okay, cut to the chase,' said Krishna impatiently.

'I will tell you what's not okay with that line of argument. In 2010, when Kingfisher was haemorrhaging, Mallya wanted more money from the bank. They refused to play ball, and when it became difficult to stand up to the pressure, the banks said, "Give us your personal guarantee", and Mallya fell right into the trap. He provided them with a personal guarantee, which was how the cookie crumbled. The bank was lending to an airline falling into an inferno, but it was their way of trying to get back the money lent!' said Junior.

'So, why did Mallya do what he did?' asked Krishna, slowly beginning to understand what had unfurled.

Larissa chipped in. 'The personal guarantee was an indication that Mallya was optimistic. However, the flames consumed India's second-largest private airline that never made profit in its lifetime.'

'The banks, the regulators and the judiciary were after him. Why should he cough up when his company takes loans, a limited liability entity?' asked Krishna.

'By the way, who faced the maximum losses?' asked Junior.

'The consortium leader, SBI. The others were mostly government-owned banks. ICICI had parachuted out of the crashing airline just in time by selling its entire Kingfisher loan to a debt fund of SREI Infrastructure Finance in mid-2012!' said Larissa.

'Smarter than State Bank,' said Krishna. The others couldn't tell if he was being sarcastic.

'Krishna, you must read the story of Vijay Mallya. A printed copy of it is in my study room. Hunt it out tonight,' said Senior.

'Yes, Sir,' said Krishna in a mock salute and ran towards the water.

THE KING IS DEAD! LONG LIVE THE KING

Never had the street fighter Vijay Mallya boxed himself into such a tight corner. Nor had he ever looked so vulnerable.

The 'King of Good Times' had tied himself into such knots that extricating him would need a Houdini's act. That was sad, because there was a time when Mallya, his smart looks and flamboyant lifestyle notwithstanding, had everything going his way. Not for nothing did he earn the moniker 'Playboy of the East'.

An alumnus of the renowned St Xavier's College in Calcutta, he inherited his dad Vittal Mallya's business, the United Breweries Group, in 1983, when he was barely 30. At one point, the group controlled a majority of the liquor business in India. Today, Kingfisher beer has a 50 per cent market share in India.[30]

Over time, the liquor baron began acquiring companies with the speed of a cheetah. He built on some, stripped others and made enemies, including Manu Chhabria, from whom he bought the liquor manufacturer Shaw Wallace. Mallya was known for his bluff and bluster. Many years ago, when questioned how the profitable company of Best & Crompton (B&C) turned sick, Mallya explained: 'When I took over, I had no idea of the company's liabilities as no due diligence audit was made. The company had an ₹30 crores hidden liability which was shown as assets. Moreover, the company included revenue pertaining to the next financial year to show profits in the current year.'[31]

So, the eventual corporate predator was a babe in the woods when he embarked on his business career.

Delivering on Kingfisher

If you thought Mallya would stick to the business he knew best, booze, you are wrong.

---

[30]Krishnan, Smruthi, 'Is Kingfisher Beer the King: When You Cover More than 50% of the Market Share?' Dutch Uncles, 16 March 2021, https://bit.ly/3BpoNGs. Accessed on 12 December 2022.
[31]*Industrial Economist*, January 1996 issue.

In 2003, he set up Kingfisher Airlines on a whim, disregarding well-meaning warnings that the airline industry was a cash-guzzler. He hired people at fat salaries and won the air-travelers' kudos for the quality of service.

To give the devil his due, he initially did deliver on what he promised—to make flying entertaining. His airline provided excellent facilities. Each seat had a TV screen where guests could surf channels according to their choice. For a domestic aircraft, it was first of its kind. He appeared on those screens welcoming guests, asking them to get in touch with him directly if they faced any issue with the service. Customers lapped it up. At the airports, you were welcomed right at the baggage-screening machine, where staff would help you get everything done smoothly.

Having a set customer service in place, Mallya decided to expand. After all, profit can come only from traffic. At some level, he must have been taken in by C.K. Prahalad's idea of 'fortune at the bottom of the pyramid'. Prahalad coined this phrase to suggest that marketers can strike gold if they target their efforts at those who are near the lower end of the income pyramid. This means that they should sell specific brands to these customers who were hitherto served by less efficient alternative products.

Mallya decided to buy Air Deccan. Captain G.R. Gopinath, the man who changed the face of air travel in Indian skies, was looking to cash out, as his low-cost carrier model was a failing proposition. Mallya hopped onto the bandwagon as a knight in shining armour.

The Failed Acquisition: Culture Clash

In one way, the acquisition made sense. It gave Kingfisher access to the Air Deccan market. It gave it a listing since Air Deccan was a listed company. It allowed Kingfisher to fly on international routes as Air Deccan met the regulatory requirement. But it also brought in its wake the latter's baggage of losses.

Mallya merged Kingfisher Airlines with Air Deccan. That done, and with all civil aviation, corporate and other tax regulations met, he renamed Air Deccan Kingfisher Red. Bravo! As Shakespeare popularly said, 'What's in a name?'

However, looked at in another way, the acquisition made no sense. First, was the low-cost model viable? Remember, Kingfisher Red (Air Deccan renamed) was just that. Two, even if it was viable, would it work in an outfit with Mallya's signature on it? This was the same man who had once purportedly said that there cannot be low-cost carriers; there can be only low-cost fares.[32] With such a mindset, was cost control ever possible? Three, if Mallya had global ambitions, would it not have been wiser for him to first crack the Indian market, consolidate its position and become profitable before going global? After all, there is a difference between Test cricket and Club cricket. To battle the big daddies of the world, you first need to become the big daddy at home.

Used as Mallya was to the high-margin liquor business, the cost-cutting culture of the low-margin airline business didn't suit him. He predictably lost, but not before borrowing tonnes of money from PSU banks.

In 2006, he got Kingfisher listed.[33] By 2011, he had nothing to show for it. The fact that he persisted is an indication that he looked to turning it around and believed that the initial losses were a part of acquiring any business. He may have deluded himself into believing that the loss was the cost of learning.

He got the Kingfisher brand valued and took loans against that. A brand is an intangible asset, and banks aren't supposed to lend on its basis. A consortium of 17 banks led by the SBI lent money to Mallya and the silver-haired business tycoon diverted crores of it to offshore tax havens.[34] As per his disclosure to the Rajya Sabha, where he was a

[32]Sinha, Saurabh, 'Low Cost Carriers Reveal High Fares', *The Economic Times*, 9 December 2010, https://bit.ly/3BrGxRx. Accessed on 12 December 2022.

[33]'Kingfisher Airlines IPO', *The Economic Times*, https://bit.ly/3ie6LjJ. Accessed on 26 November 2022.

[34]Narayan, Khushboo, 'CBI Probes How Banks Took Brand Kingfisher as Collateral', *The Indian Express*, 4 March 2016, https://bit.ly/3gzYKVC. Accessed on 26 November 2022.

member, he owned no houses. The lavish homes where he entertained people are in the balance sheets of his company.

Many believe that Mallya's work style killed Kingfisher. He was known to micromanage, ranging from the choice of cutlery onboard Kingfisher planes to hand-picking the stewardesses and their short red skirts. But, according to the jet-setting czar, the culprit was aviation turbine fuel, whose price has moved only upwards.

He may be right, but historically flying has never been for the common man.

Scattered Investments

Mallya should have perhaps stuck to liquor, as running a low-cost airlines is a serious and intricate business, and does not match the mindset of someone who holidays in yachts and spends personal time headhunting models for calendars. Worse still, he bought media companies (including Asian Age and NDTV Good Times), a football team (East Bengal) and a cricket franchisee (Royal Challengers Bangalore). In a country where cricket is religion, Mallya would surely have been attracted by the glamour of owning a team.

Since 2006, Mallya acquired the Scotland-based Whyte & Mackay Ltd for $1.2 billion and paid $109 million for the Dutch auto racing team, Spyker Formula One. He owned *Indian Empress*, a 311-foot yacht that he used in photo shoots for the annual Kingfisher calendar. He is alleged to have a fully loaded casino floating on Mondovi River in Panjim. In short, the man was here, there, and everywhere.

Sometimes, it pays to get out and move on. Mallya failed to do that.

Vijay Mallya's attire, his passion for costly yachts and swanky cars, his stays in fancy locales, and his penchant for acquiring world-heritage articles would mark him as a man of commerce. For all that, he prays every day, was a regular to Sabarimala and ensured that every jet inducted in the Kingfisher network made its maiden touchdown at the Tirupati Airport, the abode of Lord Venkateswara. Nevertheless, the gods haven't been kind to him.

Mallya's personal fortune was at one point estimated by *Forbes* magazine to be $1.1 billion.

The High and the Low

At its peak, Kingfisher Airlines was the second-largest airline in India with regards to the number of passengers. Over time, the employees' salaries fell overdue, there were mounting tax liabilities and creditors. Bankers moved the Supreme Court to stop Mallya while he owed money to them, but the man had already left with myriad suitcases in public glare.

He was accused of concealing facts about receiving $40 million from Diageo that he later transferred to his three children so as to put it beyond the reach of the courts. Mallya reportedly owed ₹9,000 crore to 17 Indian banks and was accused of fraud. He was also alleged to have routed this money to gain stakes in about 40 companies across the world.

Asylum in the UK

A two-time Rajya Sabha MP, he resigned a day before the Ethics Committee of the Upper House was to recommend his expulsion.

Facing pressure, Mallya fled to the UK on 2 March 2016, the day a few public sector banks moved the Debt Recovery Tribunal against him. Mallya has said he has been offering to make good his debts since 2016. In June 2016, a court declared Mallya a 'proclaimed offender' in connection with a money-laundering probe.[35] In January 2019, he was declared a fugitive economic offender.

By December 2016, the Enforcement Directorate (ED) attached a total of $1.8 billion worth of assets of Mallya and Kingfisher in India.[36] The ED sent letters rogatory (LR) to the US, the UK and Europe, requesting

[35]Saigal, Sonam, 'Court Declares Mallya a Proclaimed Offender', *The Hindu*, 14 June 2016, https://bit.ly/3WNbLdO. Accessed on 30 December 2022.
[36]Harly, Nicky, 'Thirteen Indian Banks Move Step Closer to Recouping £1Bn from Former F1 Boss Vijay Mallya', The National News, 19 May 2021, https://bit.ly/3DOMpFM. Accessed on 1 November 2022.

them to assist in the attachment of Mallya's over 10 foreign assets. On 3 October 2017, Mallya was arrested as part of a money-laundering case in London and released on bail. After a prolonged battle, he was declared bankrupt in a UK court, which now allowed Indian banks to carry out a worldwide freezing on Mallya's assets.

Mallya also lost his final appeal against extradition. He had filed an appeal in the UK Supreme Court in May 2020 against an extradition order to India on alleged charges of fraud and money laundering related to Kingfisher Airlines. In July 2020, Indian media reported that Mallya had offered a settlement package of ₹139.60 billion as against a total principal amount of ₹90 billion to the consortium of Indian bankers, and that this settlement was rejected.[37] In October 2020, the Indian government was told that Mallya could not be extradited due to an unspecified confidential legal matter.[38]

The Vijay Mallya case is a classic example of the collective failure of the banking system. The banks should have called him out an NPA long back. Interestingly, amidst all this, the RBI permitted the restructuring of Kingfisher.

In 2022, Mallya's attorney told the Supreme Court that he had yet to hear from his client and asked to be discharged from the case as counsel. The court agreed.

Below are the details of loans, which amount to ₹6,963 crore.[39]

Bank Name	Amount (₹Crore)
State Bank of India	1,600
Punjab National Bank	800
IDBI Bank	800

---

[37]Mahapatra, Dhananjay, 'Vijay Mallya Offers Settlement Package of ₹13,960 Crore', *The Times of India*, 17 July 2020, https://bit.ly/3sMrrBf. Accessed on 1 November 2022.
[38]'Vijay Mallya Can't Be Extradited Till Resolution of Secret Legal Matter, UK Tells India', *The Economic Times*, 9 October 2020, https://bit.ly/3C23Kde. Accessed on 26 December 2022.
[39]'Telling Numbers | Kingfisher Default Bill: ₹9,000 Crore until 2015, Largest Dues to SBI', *The Indian Express*, 14 September 2018.

Bank of India	650
Bank of Baroda	550
United Bank of India	430
Central Bank	410
UCO Bank	320
Corporation Bank	310
State Bank of Mysore	150
Indian Overseas Bank	140
Federal Bank	90
Punjab & Sind Bank	60
Axis Bank	50
Other banks	603

12

ANIL AMBANI: FROM HERO TO ZERO

'GGP, two men started at about the same time with almost the same amount of money—$4.5 billion; give or take a few. But how come one scaled the skies and the other bit the dust?' asked Junior.

'You mean, the Ambani brothers?'

'Yes, Bade Miyan and Chhote Miyan; Mukesh and Anil.'

'Well, for many reasons. Like, it could be their sheer personality. The elder was introverted, and the younger extroverted. Mukesh stayed more focussed on the job, while Anil strayed. One knew how to cut his losses; the other was fighting to prove a point. And, of course, it could also be plain luck.'

'Isn't that too simplistic a view?'

'Maybe. But that I think is the fair assessment.'

'Both Vijay Mallya and Anil Ambani failed in their businesses. Then why was Mallya pilloried, and Ambani got away from the media glare?' This time it was Krishna.

'You are right. It perhaps had to do with Mallya showing off with franchisee purchases, airline business and general haughtiness. In contrast, Anil turned up at marathons, didn't talk much and was seen as relatively sober. There were also charges that Mallya diverted corporate money, while there were no such accusations against Anil. That, of course, isn't proved.' Senior thought a bit and continued, 'In the end, the personal guarantee got them in. If the two had not given such guarantees, they may have gone scot-free.'

'Did Anil get away with a traffic offense challan in the public's eyes?' Krishna asked.

'Yup,' said Junior. 'And he also married Tina Munim, a one-time Bollywood heartthrob.'

'Now what has that to do with anything?' asked Krishna.

'Nothing really,' said GGP. 'I have a 2019 article in my attic. The two of you guys locate it and read up before the day is over.'

The man set impossible targets and the great-grandsons scurried.

THE 'MARATHON' MAN

Circa 2005, the Ambani brothers, Mukesh and Anil, penciled a family arrangement, brokered by men lettered in the world of finance. Anil, the man who runs marathons, got the new economy businesses that he wanted, viz., telecom, finance and energy. The old-economy petrochemicals operations went to Mukesh. The duo also signed a non-compete pact until 2010 to keep the ₹28,000-crore business conglomerate from in-fighting.

Let's cut to 2019.

The Anil Dhirubhai Ambani Group, or ADAG, is in tatters. The younger Ambani owes his borrowers ₹48,000 crore.[40] The group's market capitalization crashed from ₹165,917 crore in January 2008 to ₹1,687 crore in February 2019.[41] That's a 99 per cent drop! In contrast, the elder Ambani's empire has grown tenfold.

Dhirubhai built the empire from scratch, rising from a petrol pump attendant in a gas station in Yemen to heading a Fortune-500 company as chairman. At the time of his death in 2002, his sons ran the businesses together. Mukesh, a Stanford alumnus who returned midway through his MBA, became Reliance Industries Limited (RIL) chairman, while Anil, an MBA from Wharton, took on the role of managing director.

---

[40]Arun, M.G., 'Anil Ambani: The Fall of a Billionaire', *India Today*, 25 March 2019, https://bit.ly/3AKBMSr. Accessed on 27 November 2022.
[41]Ibid.

Three years into Dhirubhai's demise, the men had a bitter public fall-out that needed their mother's and super banker K.V. Kamath's intervention.

Over the years, while Mukesh grew in strength to emerge as among the 10 richest men globally, Anil reached new nadirs. His telecom venture, Reliance Communications (RCom), failed. Reliance Power was auctioned off. Reliance Entertainment disposed of Big Cinemas to slash its debt. Reliance Infrastructure sold the Mumbai city power distribution business to Adani. Reliance Capital alone, with operations in mutual funds, insurance and wealth, stayed afloat.

Anil's fall was cataclysmic.

Fall after Fall

In the 2006 partition, Mukesh walked away with a net worth of more than $4.9 billion, while Anil got $4.5 billion.[42] In 2008, Forbes named Anil the sixth richest person globally, with a wealth of $42 billion.[43] By the end of 2019, Mukesh had a net worth of $49 billion, while Anil's was a mere $2 billion.[44] In 2020, he told a London court hearing a lawsuit by three Chinese banks against RCom that he was in penury.[45]

How did it happen?

In 2015, RCom and Reliance Infratel Limited (RITL) sought two loans of ₹565 crore and ₹635 crore from SBI. Anil gave a personal guarantee to the loan amount.

On failure to repay the credit, SBI invoked the guarantee. However, before it could be enforced, the companies filed for insolvency. Consequently, all the assets of the company, and of its promoters, were

---

[42]'The Fall of an Ambani Scion', Management Study Guide, https://bit.ly/3F6ahW2. Accessed on 27 November 2022.

[43]'Mukesh vs Anil: Why Did One Ambani Brother Go Bankrupt, When the Other Became Asia's Richest Man?' Style, https://bit.ly/3OHKhUj. Accessed on 27 November 2022.

[44]'At $49 Billion, Adani Added Most Wealth in 2021', *The Economic Times*, 17 March 2022, https://bit.ly/3gzp8zb. Accessed on 27 November 2022.

[45]Browning, Jonathan, 'Anil Ambani Says His Net Worth Is Zero, Can't Pay Chinese Banks Back', *ThePrint*, 8 February 2020, https://bit.ly/3AOZtZQ. Accessed on 27 November 2022.

placed in a moratorium. The IBC did not have provisions for personal insolvency, as these rules were notified only in December 2020.

In March 2019, the audited profit of the previous year was changed from ₹1,054 crore to a loss of ₹5,549 crore. The investment in Reliance Land Private Ltd, renamed Reliance Entertainment Networks Private Ltd, was written off by ₹2,160 crore. There was not a murmur heard either from the board or the auditor. Reliance Capital had almost close to ₹1 lakh crore of exposure to lenders at some stage.[46]

In November 2021, the central bank superseded the board of Reliance Capital, and no one made a sound. With Dewan Housing Finance Corporation Ltd (DHFL), IL&FS and the like having already fallen, such news became monotonous, as citizens had become used to corporations collapsing. And in any case, people knew that Anil was a hand-shaking distance from bankruptcy. The outside liabilities of the group, as of 31 March 2021, were ₹76,000 crore and his net worth a negative ₹10,801 crore.[47]

The RBI communiqué taking over the board was too little too late, as everybody knew the ADAG's fate reasonably ahead.

The Income Tax department accused Anil Ambani of 'wilful' evasion. He was charged under sections of the Black Money (Undisclosed Foreign Income and Assets) and Imposition of Tax Act, 2015, which carries a maximum penalty of 10 years in prison and a fine. Ambani challenged the notice, arguing that the Act was passed in 2015 and that the alleged transactions occurred before that. The Bombay High Court directed that no coercive action be taken against him till 17 November 2022.

RCom, Reliance Capital, Reliance Home Finance, Reliance Infrastructure, Reliance Naval and Reliance Power are the ADAG companies. Each bit the dust. A quick review of each will help understand what went wrong.

---

[46]Ranganathan, V., 'Reliance Capital: Accommodative Accounting Aids Promoter Pilfering with Panache?' MoneyLife, 1 December 2021, https://bit.ly/3VT7Ufo. Accessed on 13 December 2022.
[47]Ibid.

Reliance Communications (RCOM)

RCom (2002) launched its smartphone in collaboration with Lenovo and chose the CDMA (Code-Division Multiple Access) platforms, while competitors Airtel and Hutch used GSM (Global System for Mobile Communication). As the industry grew, Reliance lost out, since CDMA could not support 4G when it arrived.

Once upon a time, RCom was the jewel in the ADAG crown. Anil had a 66 per cent stake, the telecom sector was booming and the company became the second largest, with a 17 per cent market share.[48] However, price wars cut the giant to size as time passed by.

Anil kept borrowing to expand his business. In 2016, after the non-compete clause ended, Mukesh got into telecom. He launched Reliance Jio and, in the process, killed RCom.

In 2017, Anil decided to sell the wireless business to Aircel and cell towers to the Brookfield Group. However, the two deals fell through. Aircel went bankrupt, and with that, the stock price of RCom sank. With stock price falling, Brookfield stepped back.

Anil tried new ways of reducing debt. The company owned land banks in Navi Mumbai, and so he drew a plan to develop and sell it. He also planned to sell off telecom-related assets to Reliance Jio. However, the deal with Jio did not happen because Jio refused to pay any dues to take over the liabilities.

That was when Anil was dragged to bankruptcy court.

One case was with a consortium of lenders led by Swiss Telecom major Ericsson. In 2013, RCom had signed an agreement with Ericsson under which the latter would manage the services of wireline and wireless network for RCom. The agreement would cover fibre and mobile infrastructure in 11 telecom circles. In 2016, trouble erupted as RCom found it difficult to pay Ericsson on time.

---

[48]'The Fall of an Ambani Scion', Management Study Guide, https://bit.ly/3F6ahW2. Accessed on 27 November 2022.

Anil settled the matter out of court but could not honour his commitment, and the creditors asked for his imprisonment. The Supreme Court threatened to do so if he didn't pay ₹5.5 billion to Ericsson India in a month. Mukesh stepped in to help his brother Anil pay.[49]

In 2019, three Chinese banks filed a lawsuit against Anil that they had lent $925 million to RCom against the bank guarantee of Anil. In 2019, RCom declared bankruptcy.[50]

Reliance Capital (RCL)

Reliance Capital, incorporated in 1986, was once the country's leading private financial company with a 20-million customer base.[51]

In July 2019, it tried to raise money by selling assets and putting its general insurance business and radio business on the block. In September, it exited its lending business while retaining the insurance units. It sold the mutual funds vertical and used the ₹6,000 crore ($860 million) proceeds to reduce outstanding debt by 33 per cent.

Infrastructure and Power

Reliance Power (now Energy) was incorporated in 1995. It had its initial public offering (IPO) sold out in less than 60 seconds on 15 January 2008, the fastest in the Indian capital market. The core business of Reliance Power is to develop, construct and maintain power projects in India and abroad. It also runs the power generation, transmission and distribution business in several parts of Maharashtra. Anil took heavy loans to buy big power plants.

[49]Rautray, Samanwaya, and Devina Sengupta, 'Anil Ambani Will Go to Jail Unless Reliance Communications Pays Up: Supreme Court', *The Economic Times*, 21 February 2019, https://bit.ly/2SefOhy. Accessed on 27 November 2022.

[50]'Three Chinese Banks Sue Anil Ambani for Failing to Repay $680-Mn Loan', *Business Standard*, 8 November 2019, https://bit.ly/3GQ2mNS. Accessed on 27 November 2022.

[51]'Reliance Capital to Expand Customer Base to 50 Million: Anil Ambani', *The Economic Times*, 4 September 2016, https://bit.ly/3u5kjjX. Accessed on 27 November 2022.

Reliance Infra had a debt of ₹127.2 billion as on March 2022.[52] Reliance Infra and Reliance Power have been defaulting on loans.[53]

Reliance Entertainment

Reliance Entertainment was incorporated in 2005. The revenue from Reliance Industries Limited's media and entertainment business was ₹47 billion in the financial year 2021.

---

[52]'Is Reliance Infrastructure (NSE:RELINFRA) Using Too Much Debt?' Simply Wall St, 31 October 2022, https://bit.ly/3GQJVce. Accessed on 27 November 2022.
[53]Reliance Power, 2nd Quarter Results, FY23, https://bit.ly/3GN8Xsr. Accessed on 27 November 2022.

13

IL&FS: INFRASTRUCTURE RUNS INTO A ROADBLOCK

'In the winter of 2018, a far-reaching calamity hit Indian banking,' said Senior with a dramatic flourish. He was sporting a pullover to guard himself from the chilly breeze. 'That year, the Infrastructure Leasing and Financial Services, longhand for IL&FS, widely perceived in the public eye as a government organization, went down the tubes. The fall shook the market and scared the public. Ten years before that, in 2008, the Lehman Brothers crisis had ripped Uncle Sam's confidence, and the US Treasury stepped in to save America's sinking mortgage-lending market. People wondered if the Indian government, too, would do so in the case of IL&FS.'

The boys hadn't seen their GGP in speech mode, and they were enthralled. They maintained silence, as the grand old man continued, 'The government did, and the government didn't. The first thing the Narendra Modi government did was sack the board that was accused of sleeping on the job. A brand new one came in, reminiscent of 2009, when Satyam erupted on our collective face. At that time, Dr Manmohan Singh did the same—pack off what remained of the sitting board and bring in its place a star-studded new one.

'Banker Uday Kotak as chairman and Vineet Nayyar as managing director were asked to helm IL&FS. Kotak was familiar with corporate India and Nayyar had played a key role in Satyam's turnaround. Also inducted were ex-banking secretary G.C. Chaturvedi, former SEBI chairman G.N. Bajpai, past Indian Administrative Service (IAS) officers Nand Kishore and C.S. Rajan, apart from sitting IAS officer, Dr Malini V. Shankar.'

As Senior paused to take a sip of water, Krishna said, 'But, GGP, what was the crisis?'

'I am getting to that. IL&FS had a total debt of ₹94,300 crore. Worse still, of the ₹18,800 crore loans advanced by IL&FS, 90 per cent had become non-performing. The company reported a loss of ₹1,887 crore in FY 2018—a steep fall from the profit of ₹142 crore a year earlier.'

Junior hurriedly chipped in. 'I read somewhere that the salaries were hiked.'

Senior did not like being interrupted, but he said nothing to that effect. 'Yes. Joke of jokes, the salary of Chairman Ravi Parthasarathy was raised by over 100 per cent during the same period, shooting him to No. 47 on Fortune India's list of 50 highest-paid executives!'

'Phew!' whistled Krishna. 'It's a telling commentary on the sense of priority of those who ran the company.'

The patriarch continued. 'Of the total ₹94,300 crore of debt, about ₹57,000 crore were owed to banks. "Where there is a scam, there is a bank" was becoming a reality. Public sector giant, SBI, had ₹3,100 crore exposure, while Bank of India had ₹3,400 crore. The private sector wasn't far behind. Both Axis Bank and Yes Bank were owed ₹800 crore and ₹2,530 crore, respectively.

'Chairman Parthasarathy and Vice Chairman Hari Sankaran were accused of evergreening loans. Managing Director Ramesh Bawa was charged with not disclosing his interest in a related party transaction. His wife Asha Kiran and daughter Akansha were directors in the two companies AAA Infosystems and AAAB Infrastructure.[54] They had entered into transactions of ₹12 crore with one of the defaulters of IL&FS Financial Services (IFIN), an IL&FS subsidiary.

---

[54] 'IL&FS Case: Bawa's Wife, Daughter Seek to De-Freeze A/Cs Citing No Mention in Charge-Sheet', *The Economic Times*, 15 July 2019, https://bit.ly/3YaWPYy. Accessed on 13 December 2022.

'Former CEO of Deloitte, Udayan Sen, the signing partner, faced trial for collusion with the management to falsify the books of accounts for the financial years 2013–14 to 2017–18. Other directors, too, were accused. The Serious Fraud Investigation Office (SFIO) alleged that the accused took favours from defaulters, including the furnishing of their apartments in Brussels in return for approving their loans.[55]

'The charge against Kalpesh J. Mehta, the statutory auditor of IFIN, is that he did not use professional scepticism. C. Sivasankaran, a Chennai-based entrepreneur, was accused of having taken loans from IFIN without intending to repay them. The Siva Group gave dud shares of Tata Teleservices as collateral to keep raising money from IFIN.'

Junior, who had done a bit of homework, asked, 'So, how did all this escape the attention of the men and women brought in to police or play chowkidars? What did the external and internal auditors, audit committees, credit rating agencies and board members comprising LIC, SBI, Abu Dhabi Investment Company and Japan's ORIX Corporation do? Did they sleep at the wheel?'

Senior smiled. 'One view is that the complicated structure of IL&FS, with several holding corporations, subsidiaries, joint ventures, associates and subsidiaries, helped the group avoid coming under the radar of the authorities. Only three of its many business entities were listed,[56] which made assessments difficult.

'To understand this more fully, you will have to get a grasp of its history. I have an international call anytime now, and it will take around 15 to 20 minutes to close it. Meanwhile, I will mail you some notes. Do go through them before we meet up again.'

'Just one quick question, GGP.' It was Krishna. 'Was this

[55]Sivasankaran, C., 'IL&FS Scam: Here Is the List of Key Players and Allegations They Are Facing', *Business Standard*, 4 June 2019, https://bit.ly/3IbxacT. Accessed on 30 December 2022.

[56]Prasad, Gireesh Chandra, 'Holding Firms Come Under Govt Scrutiny after IL&FS Crisis', *mint*, 22 October 2018, https://bit.ly/3BxpehL. Accessed on 13 December 2022.

similar to the story of Nirav Modi?'

'By no stretch of the imagination! In comparison, Modi's case was at best that of a sophisticated pickpocket. The IL&FS case is a far more nuanced story with plots and subplots that would do an author like Ravi Subramanian proud.'

Fifteen minutes later, Senior was back from his call. The boys wondered how he was still in demand at his age.

'You were talking about some history, GGP,' reminded Junior.

Krishna raised his hand. 'GGP, how big was this organization, and can you cut to the chase and tell us why it failed?'

Senior smiled. He liked the phrase 'cut to the chase', but he decided to deliver at his own pace. 'Over the years, the IL&FS group metamorphosed into a giant conglomerate with several subsidiaries, but hurt the parent company, IL&FS. Between financial years 2014–15 and 2017–18, the aggregate debt rose 44 per cent to nearly $13 billion (₹91,000 crore using ₹70/USD as exchange rate in 2018)[57] and the debt-to-net worth ratio touched a staggering 13:1. It should have been a red flag. In the same year, 2017–18, the net group loss was at ₹21 (₹147,000 crore using ₹70/USD as exchange rate in 2018) billion, while the short-term debt went up by ₹136 billion (₹13.6 thousand crore).[58]

'In hindsight, the company's business plan was flawed. It should have stuck to financing instead of jumping into execution. Infrastructure projects come in a baggage of risks: protracted implementation, delayed regulatory approvals, cost escalation and slow cash generation, to name a few, and sharp changes in the economy. And the demonetization of 2016 was in a way the last straw that broke the camel's back.

'Incidentally, in India, infrastructure financing is flawed. The closing down of development finance institutions, which lent long-

[57]Basu, Anjan, 'IL&FS and the La-La Land that is Indian Credit Rating', *The Wire*, 7 October 2018, https://bit.ly/3gMxgw1. Accessed on 28 November 2022.
[58]Basu, Anjan, 'What Triggered the Downfall of IL&FS?' *The Wire*, 12 October 2018, https://bit.ly/3gDZAAT. Accessed on 28 November 2022.

term, meant that the focus of lending shifted to commercial banks. These banks would raise money for a three- or at best five-year duration. But infrastructure projects have a long gestation period and take 10 to 15 years to show results. This mismatch between the sources and uses of funds is bound to hit, and if you notice, most NPAs are from infrastructure lending. Unless this is set right, we will be only tinkering at the margin.

'In the absence of development financial institutions, the alternative is bond markets. But India's bond markets are neither evolved, nor do they have either depth or breadth to support long-term needs.'

'But, GGP...' This time it was Junior. 'What was the board doing? Was it not its responsibility to forewarn the company about the risks of its action? Or if there were strong reservations about it, should they have not stepped back?'

Senior waved him down. 'You are right. While we will discuss board roles another day, yes, in this case, they indeed look squeamish. After all, some of our country's best minds sat on that board: R.C. Bhargava, Michael Pinto, Jaithirth "Jerry" Rao, S.B. Mathur and Rina Kamath.

'The board members had been at IL&FS for long and did not need a honeymoon period. Parthasarathy, ex-Citi, had been with IL&FS since 1987 as its CEO; Hari Sankaran, as both vice chairman and managing director for 28 years; while Arun K. Saha joined IL&FS in 1988 as the joint managing director. So had some of the other independent directors. Veteran R.C. Bhargava of Maruti Suzuki India had been there since 1990; Sunil Mathur, former LIC chairman, joined in 2005 and Jaithirth Rao, another ex-Citi person, stepped into his role in 2012.'

'Surely, the board did not come out completely clean?' said Krishna.

Senior said, 'The Risk Management Committee (RMC) is a key committee in an NBFC. It is expected to review the more important functions of a company such as asset liability management, or ALM, credit, liquidity and market risk, capital adequacy, and compliance with regulatory norms. But as per the annual report, it met only once since the financial year 2015. In contrast, IDFC, another infrastructure finance company, the RMC met 14 times from the financial years 2015 till 2018.[59]

'Worse still, the rating agencies continued to get them a "AAA" rating even when information about the IL&FS board's negligence of risk management became public news.

'In the last four years [financial year ending 2015 to financial year ending 2018], the group's net profit of ₹800 million fell to a staggering loss of ₹20.9 billion. The consolidated liabilities of the group rose from ₹680 billion in the financial year of 2015 to ₹999.5 billion by 2018, and only ₹74 billion of equity supports this mountain of debt.'[60]

Junior said, 'Did this warrant an AAA rating? Did this warrant a pay hike to directors? The directors were rewarded with a substantial hike in their remuneration, and the credit rating agencies continued with an AAA rating.'

'Ten years from now, IL&FS will be a blip on the radar. But India must develop the wherewithal to fight such attacks that terrorize its markets and makes the taxpayer foot the bill for someone else's blunders,' Senior concluded.

THE FALL OF A TITAN

This is the story of Ravi Parthasarathy, the low-profile ex-boss of IL&FS, wanted in a ₹100,000 crore scandal. He is now no more, having been felled by cancer. He helmed IL&FS, now the centre of a huge scandal.

The dubious activities of IL&FS were hidden behind a smokescreen of being a government-owned company when, in fact, it was not.

The kingpin of the scam, Ravi Parthasarathy, was the chairman of the IL&FS group, which had business activities in multiple spaces including infrastructure, finance and social amenities, all in the public–private partnership model. Conceived by M.J. Pherwani, it was established in 1987 with equity from Central Bank, UTI and HDFC to finance infrastructure ventures. Thus, it had a mixed composition of public and private sector funds. At one point, the organization had 256 group companies, comprising subsidiaries, joint venture companies and associate establishments.

IL&FS's original mandate was to provide money to establish infrastructure projects, such as toll roads, ports, power generation and distribution facilities. It imbibed an element of private sector DNA with men like Parthasarathy, ex-Citi, joining in at the top. In hindsight, the trouble began when the company, instead of restricting itself to financing a project, began getting involved in the execution process. The group raised huge loans, so much so that when the end came, on an equity capital of ₹9.83 crore, IL&FS had a debt of ₹94,000 crore.[61]

Its grandstand project, the eight-lane Delhi–Noida expressway, which was executed on land provided by the government on a 30-year lease, offered guaranteed returns of 20 per cent to equity investors. They made huge profits from the tolls they raised and had the lease extended to 100 years. The toll was stopped by the Allahabad High Court in 2016, which felt that adequate return on investment had been earned. This judgment was later upheld by the Supreme Court.

---

[61]'What Is IL&FS Crisis', *Business Standard*, https://bit.ly/3EKe3D8. Accessed on 28 November 2022.

Nobody raised a red flag, including the nominee directors. IL&FS was engaged both in the lending for and in executing projects, while these two functions are usually handled by different companies. The capital market and accounting regulators did not appear to have seen anything amiss in this. The IL&FS board members did not flag this as a conflict of interest, nor the many dubious deals made by its subsidiaries. Rating agencies, too, had nothing to say on this.

Just before the scam broke, Parthasarathy flew out to London to be treated for cancer. In a way, he was following the footsteps of Vijay Mallya. Parthasarathy took ₹26.3 crore after giving himself a 144 per cent rise in 2017–18,[62] when bankruptcy was staring the company in the face, which he must have surely been aware of. He stepped down in July 2018 on 'health grounds', and soon IL&FS began its defaults.

In July 2018, when two of IL&FS's subsidiaries failed to repay their loans, the crisis came out into the open. A couple of months later, it was becoming apparent that IL&FS might default on its various obligations, including to Small Industries Development Bank of India (SIDBI). Meanwhile, IFIN failed to meet its repayment obligations on a commercial paper.

The SFIO and the Institute of Chartered Accountants of India (ICAI) commenced their investigations. The latter declared that IL&FS had constantly drafted improper financial statements and that the two external auditors, Deloitte Haskins and Sells as well as BSR & Associates, didn't spot it.

A whistleblower, who claims to be part of the 'senior management team at Deloitte, Haskins and Sells LLP (Deloitte)',[63] alleged that Deloitte has audited the group over 10 years, and senior leadership of the firm

[62]Guha Ray, Shantanu, 'Collusion, Machinations and Alleged Links with UPA Minister: The Dark World of Ex-IL&FS Chairman Unmasked!' *Newsroom Post*, https://bit.ly/3YiAJDq. Accessed on 12 December 2022.

[63]Dalal, Sucheta, 'Whistleblower Alleges Deloitte Has Helped IL&FS Fudge Its Accounts Year after Year', MoneyLife, 10 April 2019, https://bit.ly/2Uu5qII. Accessed on 28 November 2022.

was aware of the fiscal malpractice of the IL&FS group.

The SFIO probe revealed major lapses in Deloitte's audit, and the government was quick to ban the audit major. In August 2019, the Enforcement Directorate (ED) filed a charge sheet accusing the senior management of falsifying books to continue receiving high remuneration.

At IIM Ahmedabad, where he studied, Parthasarathy was known for aggressiveness and suggestion of borderline ethical decisions in case studies. He was nicknamed 'Porki' (the northerners could not pronounce Porukki, which in Tamil means 'male goon') for this reason. 'Anyone who knows Ravi would not be surprised by the havoc they have wrought,' says an insider. Some time in 2022, IL&FS said that it sold various assets to settle ₹56,943 crore worth of debt. This represents around 93 per cent of the company's targeted debt pledged to pay off.[64]

---

[64]Statement made to one of the authors by an IIM alumnus who was Parthasarathy's classmate and wishes to remain anonymous.

14

NIRAV MODI: DIAMONDS AREN'T FOREVER

Senior, Junior and Krishna met over lunch.

'Today, I will tell you the story of the diamantaire, Nirav Modi, whose shenanigans rocked Indian banking. It spun the country's second-largest bank, PNB, into a crisis of unimaginable dimensions,' said the grand old man, Lobin Stephen Senior.

'But who is a diamantaire?' chirped Krishna. While he had a stellar vocabulary, there were still a few terms that were beyond him.

Junior was quick off the mark on his mobile, and read out from Google search, 'A diamantaire is a diamond manufacturer or a master diamond cutter. He can also be a member of diamond dealing families, well established in the upper rung of the diamond industry.'

'So, you, too, did not know the answer,' Krishna said, smirking.

Junior smiled. 'It's not important to know everything. What is important is to know where to find it.' *Savage.*

'How did the fraud happen?' Krishna was very excited to know more about the scandal.

'Well, to put it crudely, Nirav Modi's companies took fake letters of undertaking, or LoU, from PNB, and with that got banks like Andhra Bank, SBI, and others to loan him money. The money was never repaid.'

Junior turned towards his cousin, who was scratching his head in confusion. He asked his GGP, 'Can I tell him what's an LoU?'

'Please go ahead,' said Senior.

Junior finished chewing his food and, leaving the knife and fork on the plate, began explaining. 'When an Indian bank issues an

LoU, it allows its customer to raise short-term credit from another Indian bank's foreign branch. To avail the LoU, the customer must place margin money with the issuing bank. The margin money is a form of deposit. It can be for 100 per cent of the value of the LoU or a percentage of it, depending upon the relationship with the bank. Once the LoU is accepted, the foreign branch of the Indian bank transfers money to the nostro account of the issuing bank. Nostro is an account held by one bank in another bank in the other bank's home currency. The customer then uses it to pay international suppliers and service providers in foreign currency.'

'Example. Example, please,' cried out Krishna. He could not make head or tail of the technical explanation.

'Okay. Suppose your grandmother banks with PNB. Say, she has to pay X Inc. $50,000. Now, she asks PNB to help her raise credit in Singapore from Allahabad Bank. So, PNB issues an LoU to Allahabad Bank, which transfers the $50,000 to PNB's nostro account in Allahabad Bank. Note that the money is not transferred to your grandmother's personal account. From this nostro account, she pays off X Inc. By the way, before issuing the LoU, PNB would obtain from her collateral for equal value in the form of a fixed deposit or another asset.'

'Good example. Good example. So, it's like a guarantee. Like what GGP tells me, "Krishna, loan some money to Junior. I assure you he will return it on time."' Krishna imitated his GGP's voice to the last sound, setting everyone laughing.

'Brilliant,' said Junior, adding, 'Allahabad Bank earns interest on the fixed deposit, PNB a fee for facilitating the transaction and Ma-Ma a credit facility in a country where she does not have banking relationships.'

Senior sipped his lemon tea and, turning towards Krishna, remarked, 'There is another term called "round-tripping". You should know it because that is another thing Nirav Modi did.'

'What is it, GGP?'

'Let's say I make a product X and sell it to Mr A for ₹5 lakh.

A then sells it to Mr B for ₹7 lakh, and he in turn sells it to me at ₹8 lakh. Finally, I sell it to A for ₹15 lakh. Effectively, I had made a sale of ₹20 lakh (₹5 lakh plus ₹15 lakh) when it was actually only ₹5 lakh. In most cases, I, A and B are related parties, and the obvious purpose of this is to carry out deception of the turnover achieved. This practice shores up my turnover for whatever it is worth.'

'It reminds me of circular trading,' Krishna smiled.

Junior jumped up to pat his cousin. 'You pulled the words out of my mouth. Rub-off effect of having me for summer!'

Krishna wasn't sure if that was a genuine or a left-handed compliment.

Senior said, 'Before we close for the day, I must tell you about Mehul Choksi, the one the newspapers called "Mamaji". He was Nirav's uncle. Though the two weren't exactly chummy, they were co-conspirators in the PNB fraud. The CBI laid the shenanigan at ₹6,500 crore against Modi and ₹7,080 crore against Choksi.'[65]

'What happened to them?' asked Junior.

'In January 2018, the two cuckoos flew out of the nest and parked themselves in the US. In May that year, the CBI filed its first charge sheet. In the same month, Choksi relocated to Antigua, on which island he had already obtained citizenship in 2017. The PNB scam came to light subsequently.

'In March 2018, the PMLA court (court designated for handling cases under the Prevention of Money Laundering Act) issued non-bailable arrest warrants, or NBWs, against the two. It held that properties worth ₹1,210 crore, attached by the ED in the name of Choksi, are money-laundering assets.[66]

'In July 2018, the ED applied to declare Choksi a fugitive under

[65]'PNB Scam: 11 in Judicial Custody till March 28', *The Hindu*, 17 March 2018, https://bit.ly/3XCPgtp. Accessed on 27 November 2022.
[66]'Mehul Choksi's 41 Properties Worth ₹1,210 Crore Are Money Laundering Assets: Officials', *Hindustan Times*, 2 September 2018, https://bit.ly/3Toryh3. Accessed on 8 November 2022.

the Fugitive Economic Offenders Ordinance of 2018. The diamond trader contested it, saying he was outside India on business and that his medical condition did not allow him to travel. Interpol issued a red corner notice against Choksi.

'Modi was finally caught in London in 2016 for the financial fraud involving PNB and leaving India. In May 2021, Choksi went missing from Antigua and, a few days later, surfaced in Dominica. He was arrested, but a Caribbean court stayed his repatriation to India.'

Krishna looked up at the ceiling and said, 'I like diamonds. They are anyone's delight. They are lightweight, easy to carry and invaluable. There is no place you cannot hide them.'

'You planning on being a jewel thief, Brat?' his cousin teased.

Just then, a WhatsApp notification pinged. Senior had sent them one of his old articles on Nirav Modi. 'This is for today. Read it. We will catch up tomorrow with another chor.'

HOW THE COOKIE CRUMBLED

Nirav Modi (born in 1971), the celebrated jewelry designer, has been accused of being the kingpin of fraud at PNB.

A third-generation diamantaire, he was born in Gujarat and grew up in Antwerp, Belgium, where his father ran a diamond business. A dropout of Wharton School, where he met his wife, Ami, Nirav moved to India in his late teens and learnt the trade at the feet of his maternal uncle, Mehul Choksi, who inherited Gitanjali, a retail jewellery group with 4,000 stores, and ran it with elan.

Palanpuri Jain Keshavlal Modi, Nirav's paternal grandfather, had initially built the diamond business during the 1920s, starting from Gujarat and moving to Mumbai and then Singapore. He then handed it over to his two sons.

Nirav's first choice was not to become a jeweller. He attended the

Antwerp International School, wanting to be a music conductor. He went to the US to study finance and become an investment banker.

In 1999, Nirav founded Firestar Diamond, a diamond sourcing and trading company. In 2002, he started manufacturing jewellery. Three years later, he acquired Frederick Goldman, and soon he bought out both Sandberg & Sikorski and A. Jaffe, both manufacturers of engagement rings.

In 2010, he set up stores world over and opened boutiques in New York, Macau, Singapore, Beijing and London. His works were sold at Sotheby's. By now, he was on first-name terms with the movers and shakers of the film industry. They all featured in his ads: from the glamorous Priyanka Chopra and Anushka Sharma to the beautiful Lisa Haydon and Kate Winslet. In 2015, he launched his first international store at 727 Madison Avenue in New York City.

The Start: Asking for Credit

In 2011, three Nirav Modi organizations approached the Brady House branch of the PNB in Mumbai for 'buyer's credit'[67] to make payments to overseas suppliers. Thus began the scam that would soon rock India.

Two bank officers issued LoUs without proper documentation, without securing collateral and without entering the transactions in the bank's core banking software (CBS) solution, through which the bank's financial transactions are run and recorded. The RBI had mandated the banks to issue LoUs to only those parties who have existing credit relationships with a bank. In Modi's case, neither was there a credit limit nor did he ever give any margin money.

The officers briefed the overseas bank via the international cash transfer service, SWIFT. Unlike many Indian banks, PNB had not integrated its SWIFT network, which meant it was not on 'talking terms' with the trade finance module of the bank's CBS.

---

[67]Buyer's credit is a short-term credit available to an importer from overseas lenders for the purchase of goods or services. The overseas banks usually lend the importer based on the letter of comfort issued by the importer's bank.

The LoUs were cashed with the overseas branches of Allahabad Bank, Axis Bank, Bank of India, SBI and Union Bank of India.

Exposed

In January 2018, Modi's staff turned up at the same Brady House branch for further LoUs. The new gentleman staffing the forex desk told them that they should provide 100 per cent cash margin or collateral, since they did not have a sanctioned limit.

'But this had never been the standard operating practice,' the men responded.

When the bankers looked into the records, they were in for a rude shock. They found the earlier LoUs, numbering to several hundred, spread across seven years, were issued without approval and without routing through the trade finance module. All hell broke loose. The media jumped in on what was turning out to be the biggest banking scandal of the century. Charges and counter-charges flew.

Could just a couple of junior staff have masterminded such a massive rip-off? Fat chance. How were these LoUs, which were to expire in 90 days, rolled over after each expiry without detection? Does the bank not have a system of internal checks where another banker independently checks the work of one banker?

These were some of the questions raised, but more needed to be answered. Did the overseas branches not do due diligence? How could payments going out of a nostro account have been undetected for this long?

How was it possible that the nostro and vostro accounts were not reconciled? Or was that done, and people simply looked to the other side? Why did the two employees complicit in the job not have a job rotation, as banks practise?

Meanwhile, Modi, Ami (his wife and a US citizen), Nishal (his brother and a Belgian citizen) and Choksi (his uncle and now an Antiguan) fled India. Perhaps they realized the fun they had had for the last seven years could not last long.

In 2017, Forbes even estimated Modi's personal worth at $1.75 billion.[68]

Modi managed to put through 1,212 more LoUs between 2011 and 2017, skimming PNB of an estimated ₹14,000 crore. Charged by the Interpol and the Indian government for criminal conspiracy, he is being investigated for his role in the PNB fraud. He is also being sued for defrauding American entrepreneur Paul Alfonso over two custom diamond engagement rings that were laboratory-made.[69] Modi has lost the case in the UK high court, and is to be extradited to India. The court said that extraditing him won't be unjust or oppressive.

Carney's Analysis

Modi also faced round-tripping charges. According to a report prepared by John Carney, a US bankruptcy examiner, a three-carat gem was shipped at least four times between shady companies controlled by Modi over five weeks in 2011.[70] The practice of round-tripping was central to the largest fraud in Indian banking history, the report added. In one case, a diamond was sold by the US-based Firestar Diamond Inc., a Modi company and shipped to Fancy Creations Company Ltd, a Hong Kong-based shell company controlled by Modi, for $1.1 million. Two weeks later, the diamond was shipped by a partnership formed by the Modi family trust, back to Firestar Diamond for $183,000, which was its real value. The examiner pointed out that it was sent again to Fancy Creations in Hong Kong for $1.16 million shortly. And finally, A. Jaffe, a New York-based company owned by Modi, sold the diamond to a Modi shell company in the United Arab Emirates (UAE) for more than $1.2 million.[71]

[68]'Profile: Nirav Modi', *Forbes*, https://bit.ly/3OFUPDm. Accessed on 27 November 2022.
[69]Sharma, Sourabh, 'PNB Case: Nirav Modi Loses Case in UK High Court, To Be Extradited to India', *Business Today*, 9 November 2022, https://bit.ly/3GTPPsT. Accessed on 27 November 2022.
[70]Yadav, Yatish, 'PNB Fraud: US Bankruptcy Examiner Unravels Nirav Modi's Sham Business Deals through Fraudulent LoUs', *Firstpost*, 31 August 2018.
[71]Saul, Josh, 'How a Fancy Diamond Helped Nirav Modi in India's Biggest Bank

There were several instances of round-tripping, and the invoices were used to obtain LoUs from PNB, and the money deployed to fund Modi's lifestyle and settle older debts.

When PNB began legal action against Modi, he charged the bank with destroying his brand by their premature action of initiating a case against him. He offered some settlements, which the bank refused. In March 2018, Modi applied for bankruptcy in New York. The same month, the RBI scrapped the banking instrument LoU, in what can be called throwing the baby along with the bathwater.

In August 2018, the Indian government dismissed the then serving managing director and CEO of Allahabad Bank Usha Ananthasubramanian on her last day in office.[72] She had earlier been the managing director of PNB during the troubled days.

In February 2021, a UK court granted the Indian government the right to extradite Modi to India. The erstwhile diamond baron appealed against the decision to the UK High Court, claiming he would not get a fair trial in India. His appeal was rejected.

Maybe Modi and Choksi had their heart in the right place in wanting to establish India's first international luxury brand, but they went about it in a warped manner. In the process, the duo did incalculable harm to both the jewellery and the banking industry. Today, those who bought from Modi must be wondering if their purchase is genuine or fake. Banks have now become cagey about lending to diamantaires.

Perhaps if he had done an IPO instead, he would have raised money and been able to repay the bank, was one view in the market. It was planned to happen in 2018 but was cancelled, as he had fled the country.[73]

Fraud', *Business Standard*, 30 August 2018, https://bit.ly/3gAbj3r. Accessed on 27 November 2022.

[72]'Allahabad Bank MD & CEO Sacked on Last Day in Office', *The Times of India*, 14 August 2018, https://bit.ly/2OzDUls. Accessed on 8 November 2022.

[73]Mascarenhas, Rajesh, 'IPO Plans of Nirav Modi, Mehul Choksi Will Now Be "Consigned to Oblivion"', *The Economic Times*, 17 February 2018, https://bit.ly/3igJT35. Accessed on 27 November 2022.

There is a major takeaway for banks and the banking system in all this. Ever wondered why cars have brakes? If you thought it was to stop, or to reduce speed, or to avoid a collision, you are thinking like ordinary folk. Cars have brakes so that we can drive faster. Yes, it is not the accelerator but the brake that gives you the confidence to step on the pedal. The knowledge that you can hit the brakes, even when going at break-neck speed, gives you the courage to travel at that speed.

Internal control systems are to banks what brakes are to a car. The more robust the internal controls are, the faster the bank can grow without risking its survival. A set of internal controls that worked fine for decades for a particular business model in the pre-digital era may not work for another business model built around the digital economy.

As of 2022, Nirav Modi lost his appeal against extradition when the High Court of London ruled that sending him to India to face fraud and money laundering accusations was not unreasonable. Mehul Choksi's whereabouts are not known, and SEBI restricted him from accessing the securities market for 10 years.

15

DHFL: MORTGAGE MAJOR'S MUDDLE

'Today, we will look at Dewan Housing Finance Corporation Ltd, or DHFL,' announced Lobin Stephen Senior. Junior, Krishna and Larissa were gathered in his study.

'I did some research yesterday. I understand it was established long back, in 1984 to be precise,' said Krishna.

'Yup. It was the same year when an Indian prime minister was assassinated.' Junior turned to Krishna, who responded saying, 'Yeah. Indira Gandhi.'

Krishna said, 'GGP, why was the DHFL fraud so important to our country's scheme of things?'

The ex-banker adjusted his spectacles on the bridge of his nose and said, 'Because it was our second-oldest housing finance company, the oldest being HDFC. Many considered it as too big to fail.'

Junior added, 'It was important because no one tasked with regulating or keeping a watch—be it the RBI, the credit raters or the auditors—saw it coming. And when it fell, it came down like a pack of cards.'

'Hmm...' remarked Krishna. Turning to his GGP, he said, 'What do you think led to its fall?'

'Well, many things, but among the most important and the easiest to understand are that the bank borrowed for three-year periods from other banks and lent for 10-year periods to homebuyers. It meant that they were funding long-term assets with short-term borrowing. Junior, why don't you give him an example as to why this is wrong?'

Junior, always pleased to lecture, even to an audience of one, turned towards Krishna and said, 'Let's assume you have borrowed ₹750 from friends and promised to return it in a year. To that, you add ₹250 of your own money and lend the total ₹1,000 to me for three years.'

'No. Not to you. You are already an NPA,' said Krishna in all seriousness.

They all laughed. It was a pleasure to see Krishna switch between being smart and still being a child.

'I said "assume"—'

'Okay. So, a year later, I will have to settle my ₹750 to my friends, for which I may not have money unless I earn that much, while you continue to sit with my money for three years. Right?' interjected Krishna.

'Bang on.'

'And if this pattern of borrowing short-term and lending long-term happens significantly, it could destroy a company.'

'Right. But then, why do companies do it?'

'Good question, Brat. One reason is that short-term borrowing costs less than long-term borrowing. Imagine at what rate you would lend to me if it's a three-year period and if it's a five-year period.'

'Again, a loan to you? Well, if it's five years, obviously higher. Because I wouldn't know where you would be five years from now, so the risk is higher.'

'Precisely. Short-term loans are less risky and so cost less interest. Naturally, companies fall for it. They think they can earn during the intervening period. And of course, for some people, the risk involved gives them an adrenaline rush.'

At this point, Senior stepped in. 'While this was at the heart of the crisis, it was also that a lot of money was lent to shell companies and round-tripped. In the end, the depositors did get their money back, but the trust in the system was deeply hurt.'

'But, GGP, why do these guys do it? Do they think they will

never get caught? And what were the auditors and board doing?'

'These are all fair questions, my boy. They involve issues of ethics and morality. We will have to reserve that for another day, another time. As to what the auditors and board were doing, we will talk about it after going through the scandals. Remember, I am not justifying their role, but I have been on boards and know what we are up against.'

Junior closed the discussion, saying, 'If you say so, it must be true.'

'What were the other reasons for the debacle?' It was Krishna.

Junior, who had studied this topic at Harvard, volunteered to answer. 'DHFL was an NBFC. Do you remember banks were asked to lend to NBFCs, something we picked up in one of our earlier conversations? So, along with bank money, DHFL raised funds through bonds and other debt instruments that were subscribed to by retail investors.

'A web magazine, called *Cobrapost*, laid bare the charge that DHFL lent to shell companies that were linked to the promoters of the DHFL group in a post dated 29 January 2019.[74] That's when the crisis first came under the public glare, in 2019, although the company had been playing truant since 2010. The post also claimed that the loan was against inadequate security. This money was used to acquire assets across the world. When the loans became NPAs, retail investors were left holding the baby.'

The boys agreed they would read up an article on DHFL that Larissa had shared late the previous night.

---

[74]Bahal, Annirudha, 'Dewan Housing Finance Corporation Limited: The Anatomy of India's Biggest Financial Scam', *Cobrapost*, 29 January 2019, https://bit.ly/2UkHmTW. Accessed on 28 November 2022.

DHFL: THE HOUSE THEY BUILT ON QUICKSAND

In 1984, R.K. Wadhawan established DHFL. The company was headquartered in Mumbai as an NBFC to provide home finance for low income group and middle income group households. Over time, DHFL grew, such that it was among the top 50 financial companies in India.

Thirty-five years later, in June 2019, all hell broke loose, leaving ordinary citizens stunned. Rating agencies, such as CRISIL and ICRA, downgraded DHFL's Commercial Paper to 'D', which meant they were no longer expecting the company to repay its short-term debts.

It was not that these men from the rating agencies, mandated to watch companies from the sidelines, had done some stellar work. They merely picked the market grapevine and acted on it. They were possibly busy snoring when the early signs became visible. To cut a long story short, the day after the downgrade, DHFL defaulted on its commercial paper (CP), sending the market into a tizzy.

There is a history to this.

In 2018, when IL&FS went belly-up, banks stopped lending to NBFCs. The action led to a crisis, and DHFL was among the affected parties. The IL&FS situation meant fewer buyers of DHFL's CPs. The NBFC was also reeling under high NPAs. It dealt with long-term housing loans, and borrowed from insurance companies and mutual funds by issuing CPs.

As a result, the NBFCs got into short-term borrowing to finance their long-term lending. Such action is against the basic tenet of money management and is taught on the first day of a finance class in any B-school. Perhaps the NBFCs did not have a choice as lenders weren't easily forthcoming. Perhaps they thought that the tide would turn and that the current scenario was temporary.

The company started borrowing from anyone who was willing to lend: ₹50,000 crore was from banks and ₹30,000 crore from the LIC and others.[75] Under Indian law, once there is a default, rating agencies

---

[75]'India's Biggest-Ever Bank Loan Fraud: All You Need to Know about ₹ 34,000-Crore

have to downgrade the instrument to 'D'. The downgrade meant that mutual funds were hit hard, as they had to mark down all DHFL papers 75 per cent—meaning they had to reduce the value at which the investments were shown in the books, even if it is not the instrument that the company defaulted on. UTI Mutual Fund wrote off the entire debt, indicating that they expected nothing back from the company.

The group's claim that this was just a liquidity crisis and not a solvency issue had very few takers. If it were a liquidity crisis, they just had to raise money to pay off liabilities. But a solvency crisis meant a poor business model, inability to meet a payment obligations and hence the high possibility of bankruptcy.

In January 2019, *Cobrapost* had accused DHFL of using shell corporations to siphon off ₹31,000 crore for the personal gains of the Wadhawans.[76] The investigative journalism group had alleged political donations worth crores of rupees, violating Section 182 of the Companies Act, 2013. Despite the allegations, rating agencies had stuck with the high safety rating for the financial instruments issued by DHFL.

With the downgrade in June, the DHFL stock price crashed, wiping off 97 per cent of the capitalization. On its part, the company offered to repay investors fully.

In October 2019, the ED raided DHFL offices and found links to money-laundering activity. The trail of one of the loans led to Mumbai gangster Iqbal Mirchi. A month later, the RBI fired the company board, citing inadequate governance and defaults on payment obligations. It also initiated insolvency proceedings against DHFL, the first NBFC to go through a corporate insolvency resolution process.

In January 2020, Wadhawan was arrested under PMLA, 2002, but was released on bail the following month. In March 2021, the CBI

DHFL Scam', *Outlook*, 24 June 2022, https://bit.ly/3VvzNcW. Accessed on 28 November 2022,
[76]Sarkar, Gaurav, 'Cobrapost Exposé Finds DHFL Promoters Siphoned over ₹31,000 Crore of Public Money', NewsLaundry, 29 January 2019, https://bit.ly/2SjJfTS. Accessed on 12 December 2022.

accused the Wadhawans of siphoning off the welfare subsidy fund of the Pradhan Mantri Awas Yojana by creating 260,000 fake home loan accounts under the same scheme.[77]

Acquisition

After the scandal broke, bidders for DHFL included Piramal Group, the US-based Oaktree Capital Management, the Hong Kong-based SC Lowy and Adani Group. These companies were interested in DHFL because despite the distressed assets, taking over would mean acquiring a fully functional housing finance company. The mortgage major had 570 branches, 2,179 permanent employees and a strong presence in tier-2 and tier-3 cities, where a real estate boom is expected to take place in the near term.[78]

In 2020, Deloitte Haskins & Sells, the company's statutory auditors, resigned. DHFL went on record saying that it will be unable to meet its repayment obligations. The company said that it had ₹30,000 crore of retail loans through securitization to meet financial obligations.[79]

Usually, the assets are pooled in securitization, and a special purpose vehicle (SPV) issues tradable securities to buy assets. But under direct assignment, no SPV is made, and the company transfers assets to other companies through an assignment deed. Under this arrangement (direct assignment), collecting loans still lies with DHFL. Will this affect how other creditors will respond to payment calls?

DHFL practised imaginative accounting that kept it artificially alive. For instance, in the results of March 2019, cheques worth ₹16,487 crore[80]

[77]'CBI Books DHFL over Fake Accounts Created in PMAY', *mint*, 24 March 2021, https://bit.ly/3AQ34XY. Accessed on 28 November 2022.

[78] Iyer, Priyanka, 'Why Are Bidders Willing to Shell Out More for DHFL', ETNowNews. com, 5 December 2020, https://bit.ly/3WqjDIY. Accessed on 26 December 2022.

[79]'May Not Be Able to Meet Financial Obligations in Near Future: DHFL', *The Economic Times*, 8 August 2019, https://bit.ly/3PnwCC3. Accessed on 12 December 2022.

[80]Merwin, Radhika, 'DHFL Crisis: The "Hidden" Issues No One Is Talking About', *The Hindu BusinessLine*, 6 December 2021, https://bit.ly/3OJ3FAr. Accessed on 28 November 2022.

received from borrowers were recorded as receipts, although they had not been deposited. In subsequent quarters, it was reversed. It indicated that there were lacunae in the documentation for a value of ₹20,750 crore.[81] The auditors stated that they could not obtain sufficient evidence to support the values of the loans.

Forensic auditor Grant Thornton identified ₹2,151 crore undervaluation in the sale of DHFL stake in Pramerica Life Insurance Ltd.

Worse news followed. At the end of March 2019, India Ratings reported that the NHB, the government-run agency that promotes housing finance institutions, had massive exposure to DHFL and Punjab and Maharashtra Cooperative (PMC) Bank to the extent of ₹2,435 crore and ₹1,754 crore, respectively![82]

The NCLT approved the Piramal Group's bid for the bankrupt DHFL subject to the final ruling from the National Company Law Appellate Tribunal (NCLAT) and the Supreme Court's judgment on the R.K. Wadhawan matter.

In September 2021, the Piramal Group announced it had, through Piramal Capital and Housing Finance Ltd, completed the takeover of DHFL, and discharged the consideration to the creditors.

Investigations by the SEBI, ED and CBI have linked the Yes Bank scam to the Wadhawans and the Kapoors. As of December 2022, unhappy with the resolution strategy, DHFL's fixed deposit holders have moved to the apex court requesting a full reimbursement of their claims.

[81]Dugal, Ira, 'Questions Raised by DHFL's Unaudited Earnings Release', *BQ Prime*, 15 July 2029, https://bit.ly/3u8bbuU. Accessed on 28 November 2022.
[82]'NHB Exposure in DHFL at ₹2,435 Crore', *The Economic Times*, 9 October 2019, https://bit.ly/3UM7ZjG. Accessed on 13 December 2022.

16

NO TO YES BANK

In the evening, Senior opened the discussion, 'Today, there is an important tennis match. We have the first Indian making it to the Wimbledon singles final.'

Junior said, 'Yes, a rookie, Sandy Mathias. Coming up from the qualifying event.'

'What do you think are his chances?'

'Well, history is on his side. In 1985, unseeded Boris Becker came from the qualifying rounds to beat Kevin Curren to become the first floater in history to pick the prestigious lawn tennis trophy.'

'You think our man will also be able to do it?'

'I don't know, but in case he does, I don't want to miss out watching it.'

'What are you hinting at?'

'I am saying that we defer our discussion on Yes Bank to tomorrow.' Junior looked sheepish as he said this.

'Well, I will do one thing better. I will send you a brief note that was prepared on the bank. You read that up. It's self-explanatory, now that you know how several of these rackets worked.'

'And in case we have doubts, we come back to you tomorrow?'

'Yup.'

'Bingo.'

Krishna McKenzie, who had all along been quiet, let out a loud squeal of joy. Sandy Mathias was his favourite. 'Yup. Tomorrow,' he said, and ran without a second look.

As the night would show, Mathias, the 18-year-old tall, ebony-skinned Indian, would flatter to deceive. Two sets up and serving with three championship points, nervousness hit him. In the most miraculous Houdini act ever, the defending champion would outsmart the talented rookie to pick up another trophy.

RISING LIKE A PHOENIX

This is the story of a failed bank. It grew up in an era where greed, lies, deceit, selfishness and crony capitalism were familiar sentiments. Where regulators failed, auditors were clueless, the board was ineffective and rating agencies turned a blind eye.

On 21 November 2003, brothers-in-law Rana Kapoor and Ashok Kapur incorporated Yes Bank. Headquartered in Mumbai, the bank operated in treasury, corporate banking and retail banking. While Ashok wanted to drive growth steadily, Rana was in a tearing hurry. For a while, it all worked and awards came in rapid succession.

In 2005, the bank won the Corporate Dossier Award from the Economic Times. In 2006, it received the Financial Express Awards for India's Best Banks. In 2008, it was top-ranked in the Business Today-KPMG Best Banks Annual Survey.[83] Soon, it was a part of the Sensex, and over time, emerged as the country's fourth-largest bank.

Then 26/11 happened, and in the dastardly shoot-out, the bullets of the terrorists felled Chairman Ashok Kapur.

Rana now had an unfettered charge and ran the bank like a man possessed. The bank's structure was way too centralized for anyone's good, and it was lending all over the place. Those that others wouldn't touch with a bargepole would turn to Yes Bank, and ironically, the bank mastered the art of always responding with a 'Yes'. Such was the madness in lending that its credit growth in calendar year 2017 outpaced the banking industry. This should have alarmed everyone,

---

[83]Yes Bank Ltd: Company History, *Business Standard*, https://bit.ly/3OWJzTr. Accessed on 28 November 2022.

coming as it did when investments in the economy were falling.

But Rana had a trailblazing CV. A graduate from Shri Ram College of Commerce (1977), he picked an MBA from Rutgers University (1980). He first interned at Citi Bank, then worked for 15 years at Bank of America and later in ANZ Grindlays, where he dreamed of one day having his own bank.[84] A fixer who knew the powers that be, he was cocky. In 2018, politicians, film stars and corporate honchos were at his eldest daughter's wedding reception. That was the kind of network he built. Most journalists were in awe of his smooth-talking ways, and he engaged with them. The media houses ate out of his hand, thanks to deals and big-ticket advertisements.

Flashpoint

Yes Bank lent vast amounts to ADAG, Cox & Kings, Café Coffee Day, DHFL, Essel, Housing Development and Infrastructure Limited (HDIL), IL&FS and Jet Airways, all of which failed. When you see those names today, you are shocked. Why was it done? Apparently, Rana believed that the economy would bounce back sooner than later, and by picking a 10 per cent upfront fee, he could shore up his profit and loss account. But when his borrowers failed, it was natural that Yes Bank, too, would follow, evergreening of loans notwithstanding.

Rana was asked by the RBI to step down in September 2018. His antics of trying to stay by hook or crook didn't cut ice with Governor Urjit Patel.[85]

In November 2018, as the screw tightened, Chairman Ashok Chawla stepped down. Other directors followed suit. Vasant Gujarathi, O.P. Bhatt and Rentala Chandrashekhar exited in quick succession. In January 2020, ICAI former chief and Yes Bank board member Uttam Prakash

[84]Karnik, Madhura, 'Once an Intern at Citibank, Yes Bank's Rana Kapoor Is Now India's Newest Banking Billionaire', Quartz, 23 January 2013, https://bit.ly/3ilWj9X. Accessed on 28 November 2022.

[85]'Everything You Need to Know About the Yes Bank Collapse, Rescue and Prospects', ThePrint, 9 March 2020, https://bit.ly/3heTK9t. Accessed on 12 December 2022.

Agarwal resigned after flagging corporate governance issues. Mark it; he was head of the Audit Committee.

In the last quarter of 2019, Rana, who had once sworn that he would never sell his bank's share, sold a part of his stake. Over the next year, he sold almost the whole lot, excepting for 900 shares. Qualified institutional investors had bought into the claims and saw their money go down the drain by 65 per cent within a single month.

Even if the regulators did not, the markets read these developments.

The deposit to loan ratio had fallen below one. The bank had lent ₹2.25 trillion as of 30 September 2019, and its deposits were ₹2.1 trillion.[86] The Provision Coverage Ratio (PCR), too, had fallen. The bank needed money to provide for NPA, but CASA (current account and savings account) ratio was heading south, falling to 33.1. CASA ratio stands for current and savings account ratio, which is the ratio of deposits in current and saving accounts to total deposits. Since these amount cost less by way of interest, a low ratio indicates that the bank does not have access to this form of borrowing. Consequently, it meant that cheap forms of financing were no longer available, but costlier finance, too, was difficult to come by as companies were unwilling to invest money in Yes Bank due to a staggering contingent liability of ₹6.7 lakh crore. That was 1.8 times its balance sheet size![87]

The bank's NPA doubled between April and September 2019 to touch ₹17,134 crore. There was no stopping the bleed. As of March 2020, the gross NPA was ₹28,609 crore (15.41 per cent) and net NPA ₹9,813 crore (5.88 per cent). By the end of June 2020, the Common Equity Tier 1 and Tier 1 capital ratios were 6.48 per cent and 6.63 per cent, respectively, against the minimum requirements of 7.375 per cent and 8.875 per cent, respectively.

As share prices plummeted from ₹400 in 2018 to ₹16.60 in 2020, rating agencies downgraded Yes Bank instruments.

[86]'Yes Bank Crisis – Causes, Consequences & Measures', IAS Express, 12 April 2020, https://bit.ly/3C0RSbu. Accessed on 26 December 2022.
[87]Ibid.

Various whistleblowers' complaints came in, some were acted upon, and some were not. Several of the protests turned true, especially those relating to employee payouts.

In March 2020, Rana was arrested for alleged financial irregularities and purported kickbacks. In January 2021, the ED picked him for a money-laundering case linked to a ₹4,300 crore fraud in PMC Bank.[88]

What were the directors doing? Possibly, they were not reading the documents or did not take their job seriously.

Restructure

In March 2020, the RBI imposed a 30-day moratorium on Yes Bank—which meant that depositors could not withdraw money during that period subject to some conditions on the amount and the number of withdrawals—and Prashant Kumar, the chief financial officer at SBI, was appointed as the administrator. To control the financial burden, the deposit withdrawals were capped at ₹50,000 per day and ₹5 lakh per person. Earlier, in the three months starting October 2019, the deposits fell by ₹44,000 crore as depositors withdrew their money.[89]

As per the government reconstruction scheme, SBI was to acquire 49 per cent of the restructured capital. Private players like ICICI, Kotak Mahindra, HDFC, Federal Bank, etc., lent a helping hand and invested as well. Further, it was agreed that SBI could not reduce its stake below 26 per cent, and other investors could not withdraw more than 25 per cent of their investments in the next three years. The plan proposed was that the existing shareholders, who owned 2.55 million shares, would end up with around an 11 per cent stake in the company after the reconstruction. Other players chipped in with ₹9,600 crore—the balance amount required to rebuild the bank.

The employees were assured of the same remuneration for at least

[88]'ED Arrests Yes Bank Co-Founder Rana Kapoor in Fresh Money Laundering Case', *The Hindu*, 27 January 2021, https://bit.ly/3VO79Ed. Accessed on 12 December 2022.
[89]Saha, Manojit, 'Explained: Why Did Yes Bank Have to be Bailed Out?' *The Hindu*, 8 March 2020, https://bit.ly/3iUcKdE. Accessed on 12 December 2022.

one year, and the offices were allowed to function as before. The RBI loaned ₹10,000 crore to Yes Bank against government securities.

Years ago, Global Trust Bank had to be bailed out with a merger with Oriental Bank of Commerce (now merged with PNB). The government has always argued and rightly so, that banking rests on only one pillar, namely trust. And it believes that banks should not be allowed to fail. And Yes Bank had lost the trust of the people.

17

PMC BANK: UNCOOPERATIVE BANKS

'GGP, you have been talking to us about the public sector and private sector banks. Are these the only two categories to go down the drain, or is there a third category?'

Junior wasn't very pleased with words like 'drain', so he scowled at Krishna but kept his wisdom to himself.

'Well, there is a category called Urban Co-operative Banks, or UCBs. They are generally located in urban and semi-urban areas,' replied Senior. 'Some time in the closing years of the nineteenth century, inspired by the success of these experiments in Britain and Germany, such institutions were set up in India. The UCBs focussed on attracting savings from middle- and low-income urban groups and providing credit to their members. Interestingly, during the banking crisis of 1913–14, when 57 joint stock banks collapsed, deposits were withdrawn from joint stock banks and placed in UCBs, indicating that people felt these were safer.

'In 1966, cooperative banks were brought under the purview of the Banking Regulation Act of 1949 and within the ambit of the RBI's supervision. Banking-related functions, such as licensing, area of operations, interest rates, etc., were to be governed by the RBI, while registration, management, audit, liquidation, etc., were to be governed by state.

'Most of these banks are concentrated in Gujarat, Karnataka, Maharashtra and Tamil Nadu.' Senior stopped to have a sip of water. The doctors had told him to have at least six glasses a day.

Krishna felt this was the time to stop his great grandfather.

'GGP, it looks like UCBs are drab. No drama, no excitement, no-nothing.'

Junior smiled and said, 'Krishna is looking for frauds and resolutions.'

Krishna beamed, and Senior smiled indulgently. 'For that, we have to jump to 1984.'

'Again, 1984?' screamed Krishna. He had read George Orwell's *Nineteen Eighty-Four*, understood nothing, and had gone to town saying it was a stupid book.

Junior ignored him. 'In 1984, Punjab and Maharashtra Cooperative Bank, or PMC Bank, started in a super-small room in Mumbai. By 2018, it was named the best bank in the over ₹2,000 crore capital category. In 2019, it was operating in six states and had 137 branches with a deposit base of ₹11,617 crore. It boasted a total income of ₹1,297 crore and a hefty profit of ₹100 crore.'[90]

'I am waiting for the sting in the tail,' said Krishna.

Senior smiled at the sarcasm. 'In September 2019, PMC Bank crashed because of a massive fraud.'

'What! Within one year of being named the best bank?' Krishna was incredulous.

'Unfortunately, yes.'

'How did this fraud come to light?'

'Well, when RBI inspectors found that the bank had created 44 fictitious accounts to hide ₹4,355 crore of loans to the bankrupt HDIL.'

Junior chipped in. 'It was clear manipulation as the Core Banking Solution had also been tampered with, and the accounts were accessible only to a select few.'

'How do you know? How do you know?' asked Krishna, a tad angry that Junior knew more than him.

Senior asked Junior to fill in the gaps.

---

[90]Singh, I.P., 'Sikhs of Bombay Helped Launch PMC Bank in 1984', *The Times of India*, 12 October 2019, https://bit.ly/3iiOiCq. Accessed on 28 November 2022.

'HDIL was a real estate development company, which went to the NCLT, and subsequently declared bankruptcy,' said Junior.

Krishna was foxed. 'Now, are you introducing another company in this story? Are you trying to take revenge on me?'

'Yes, I am introducing a key player in the plot. And no, I am not taking revenge on you.' Junior was getting slightly irritated with these meaningless interjections. 'PMC Bank lent ₹2,500 crore to HDIL in gross violation of RBI norms. Under those regulations, a cooperative bank cannot lend more than 15 per cent of its capital to a company and, in the case of a group entity, the upper limit is 40 per cent. The PMC Bank loan was a good 237 per cent of its total capital. When HDIL defaulted, the aggregate of principal and interest was ₹4,355 crore.'[91]

Krishna had his eyes wide open. 'And the RBI looked the other way.'

'Worse still. The PMC Bank did not declare the loan as an NPA. And the most interesting part is that in the financial year of 2019, the bank disclosed NPA percentage was only 2.19.'

Krishna whistled under his breath. Senior did not like it one bit, and clicked his tongue in annoyance.

'Sorry. Sorry. But I was stumped. I am sure the fraud must have been going on for several years.'

'You are right,' said the octogenarian. 'It was going on for seven years. The bank also lent to other corporates, who defaulted, and these defaults were hidden under 21,049 dummy accounts.'

'Twenty-one thousand and forty-nine,' Krishna recited the words almost reverently, bowled over at the size of the sum.

[91]Adhikari, Anand, 'PMC Bank Lent to over Half a Dozen HDIL Entities in 2017', *Business Today*, 30 September 2019, https://bit.ly/3APseFO. Accessed on 28 November 2022; Sinha, Ankita, 'How a Three-Decade Relationship with HDIL Cost PMC Bank 4,355 Cr', *The Quint*, 9 October 2019, https://bit.ly/3F8YVkh. Accessed on 28 November 2022.

Junior took over. 'The HDIL promoters, Rakesh Wadhawan and his son Sarang Wadhawan, were arrested on 3 October 2019. The following day, Joy Thomas, former managing director of PMC Bank, was taken into custody.

'Sometime in September 2019, the bank started defaulting on its deposits, and the RBI walked in to freeze withdrawals first beyond ₹50,000 and later ₹1 lakh. It left nine lakh depositors fuming.'

'This now looks like a template. I am sure the bank numbers were looking bad,' Krishna told no one in particular.

'On the contrary,' said Junior, 'they were looking good. It had produced a super-healthy audited balance sheet on 9 September 2019. The total income was ₹1,297 crore, and net profits ₹100 crore. While CAR stood at 12.62 per cent, the bank's savings rate was 4 per cent per annum and the deposit rate 7.5 per cent.'[92]

'Did none of the regulators have the slightest clue of what was happening?'

Senior responded, 'The RBI listed financial irregularities, internal control and systems failure, and under-reporting of lending as the causative factors.

'In June 2020, the central bank doubled the withdrawal limit to ₹1 lakh, allowing 84 per cent of the depositors to withdraw their entire account balance. In June 2021, it approved Unity SFB (Unity Small Finance Bank) to take over PMC Bank. This was a joint venture between Centrum Financial Services and Resilient Innovations Pvt. Ltd, which runs payments company BharatPe.'

'The RBI's resolution plan for PMC Bank hurt the depositors big time, and they indirectly took a haircut,' Junior added.

'Why, what happened?' asked Krishna.

'I am mailing you a brilliant article that was shared with me, and from which I made some jottings. A heads-up: retail

---

[92]Adhikari, Anand, 'What You Must Know about Punjab and Maharashtra Co-Operative Bank', *Business Today*, 24 September 2019, https://bit.ly/3EGGEJL. Accessed on 28 November 2022.

depositors would receive up to ₹5 lakh immediately. Sums beyond that were staggered repayments stretching to 10 years, without interest for the first five years.'

'What!' said Krishna, who ran a small moneylending business of his own among his friends.

'After the fifth year, they would be eligible for 2.75 per cent interest annually,' said Senior. In his mind, he recalled having placed ₹10 lakh in the disgraced bank. 'The institutional depositors received a worse deal. Read up my mail and we will catch up tomorrow.'

Krishna turned to Junior. 'Do you know the numbers?'

'For institutional depositors, 80 per cent were to be converted into Perpetual Non-Cumulative Preference Shares, with a dividend of 1 per cent per annum. The remaining 20 per cent were to be converted into equity warrants of Unity SFB at a price of ₹1 per warrant. These equity warrants would further be converted into equity shares of the Unity SFB at the time of the IPO, when it went for one.'

'What a shame indeed! These are worthless investments,' said Krishna disbelievingly. Had he known his great grandfather had ₹10 lakh blocked in the bank, his disbelief would have turned into disgust.

PMC BANK
(RANGANATHAN V., 2021)[93]

On 22 November 2021, a scheme of rehabilitation of the Punjab and Maharashtra Cooperative (PMC) Bank has been put out for public comments by the Reserve Bank of India (RBI). The depositors, who were desperately waiting for justice, have been shell-shocked by the terms of the new plan.

[T]he headline shocker is that a deposit, which is in excess of Rs5 lakh is not payable immediately; a deposit of say Rs10 lakh will take four years to get redeemed; and a deposit of say Rs25 lakh will be liquidated over 10 years only.

The injustice is not limited to the elongated period but made worse many times over with no interest being paid for the first five years and a piddly 2.75% interest per annum thereafter!

A new entity named Unitus Small Finance Bank Ltd, a special purpose vehicle (SPV) created by an interested investor, acquires the business of PMC Bank from an appointed date to be notified.

The picture created, of the deposits getting fully paid, is patently misleading. To imagine a premier regulator resorting to camouflage is most obscene!

The relevant clauses of the terms of repayment of the non-institutional depositors are extracted for ready reference.

(c) The transferee bank will pay—

(I) the amount received from the Deposit Insurance and Credit Guarantee Corp (DICGC) to all the eligible depositors of the transferor bank, which would be an amount equal to the balance in their deposit accounts or Rs5 lakh, whichever is less, in accordance with the rules of distribution of such amounts;

---

[93]Ranganathan V., 'PMC Bank: Scheme of Subterfuge Stuns as Dubious Dispensation Ditches Despondent Depositors', MoneyLife, 25 November 2021, https://bit.ly/3YvNUBh. Accessed on 19 December 2022. (Reproduced with permission from the author).

(II) at the end of two years from the appointed date, over and above the payment already made, an additional amount equal to the balance in their deposit account or Rs50,000, whichever is less, on demand only to the retail depositors of the transferor bank,

(III) at the end of three years from the appointed date, over and above the payments already made, an additional amount equal to the balance in their deposit account or Rs1 lakh, whichever is less, on demand only to the retail depositors of the transferor bank,

(IV) at the end of four years from the appointed date, over and above the payment already made, an additional amount up to the balance in their deposit account or Rs3 lakh, whichever is less, on demand only to the retail depositors of the transferor bank.

(V) at the end of five years from the appointed date, over and above the payment already made, an additional amount up to the balance in their deposit account or Rs5.50 lakh, whichever is less, on demand only to only the retail depositors of the transferor bank.

(VI) the entire remaining amount of deposits (after making payment as mentioned in clause (I), (II), (III), (IV) and (V) above in the accounts of the retail depositors of transferor bank after 10 years from the appointed date, on demand. (d) The interest on any of the interest-bearing deposits with the transferor bank shall not accrue after 31 March 2021 except in the manner provided hereunder. No further interest will be payable on the interest bearing deposits of transferor bank for a period of five years from the appointed date.

In respect of balances in any current account or any other non-interest bearing account, no interest shall be payable to the account holders, Provided further that interest at the rate of 2.75% per annum shall be paid on the retail deposits of the transferor bank which shall be remaining outstanding after the said period of five years from the appointed date. This interest will be payable from the date after five years from the appointed date.

In a nutshell, a deposit above Rs5 lakh that does not enjoy the cover of DICGC is paid in instalments over a period of 10 years. No interest would accrue for the first five years and interest at 2.75% per annum is payable from the expiry of the fifth year only. This structure is a disguised way of making the depositors bleed.

In a simple example of a depositor with Rs25 lakh of deposit outstanding, the formula given in the scheme results in a financial loss of about Rs7 lakh over the 10 years assuming that the depositor could have earned interest at 7% per annum on the outstanding amount.

Is it not a subterfuge to create a false impression that the deposits are finally repaid in full with no loss? It would have fallen foul of the regulator's own rules if a commercial bank or a non-banking finance company (NBFC) were to advertise a scheme of a similar nature seeking deposits on these terms of repayment stating that it is a capital guaranteed scheme!

The institutional deposit-holders have the most outlandish dispensation. The condition is extracted below:

On and from the appointed date, 80% of the uninsured deposits outstanding (aggregate in various accounts) to the credit of each institutional depositor of the transferor bank shall be converted into perpetual non-cumulative preference shares (PNCPS) of transferee bank with a dividend of 1% per annum payable annually.

After ten years from the appointed date, the transferee bank may consider additional benefits for such PNCPS holders either in the form of providing a step-up in coupon rate or a call option, upon receipt of approval from the Reserve Bank.

(f) The remaining 20% amount of the institutional deposits will be converted into equity warrants of transferee bank at a price of Re1 per warrant. These equity warrants will further be converted into equity shares of the transferee bank at the time of the initial public offer (IPO) when the transferee bank goes for public issue. The price for such conversion will be determined at the lower band of the IPO price.

To further expand on the matter and bring out the anomaly of this structure, it is questionable if preference shares can be perpetual. A typical company cannot issue such an instrument. The most outlandish step is to fix a coupon rate of 1%, which does not reflect any prevailing rate in the Indian financial markets where even government borrowings are 6%+!

The PMC Bank scheme has very poor disclosures of assets like cash balance and government securities that are key to any bank's functioning. As of 31 March 2019, the Bank had cash of Rs708 crore, balance with scheduled banks of Rs409 crore and government and other securities of over Rs3,000 crore. Isn't it essential in public interest to amplify how the valuation has been done to justify the present terms of paying the depositors?

Most importantly, there is no guarantee of any sort that money will be returned in the stated period. Small finance banks don't have a tested business model and, given the volatility in the financial sector, 10 years is too long to assume that the Bank will exist as it is. It can transform in an acquisition or merger and the new owner will not be bound by these terms.

18

LAKSHMI VILAS BANK: THE HOUSE OF WEALTH

'GGP, in all our stories so far, we haven't talked about a single South-based bank or entrepreneur who took the system for a ride. Are the Southerners good as hell?' asked Krishna.

'Where does Vijay Mallya come from, dunce?' asked Junior.

'Okay, okay. Got it. Whom are we talking about today?'

Senior slowly got into speech mode. 'Well, today we are discussing our final scandal. This one is about the Lakshmi Vilas Bank, or LVB. It is a Tamil Nadu-based bank, and lived all of 94 years before being caught in a scam. By the way, as usual I will, sometime today, forward you a note on the bank for you to read before we meet up next time.'

He waited for his great-grandsons to settle down and continued the narration. 'On 17 November 2020, the RBI imposed a month-long moratorium on the 94-year-old bank. A moratorium is finance's equivalent of an intensive care unit, and LVB's financial health required this treatment. It was a fall from grace, but while many were stumped and depositors had their hearts in their mouths, it did not come as a surprise to those with a ringside view.

'In a press release that day,[94] the RBI spoke about how the bank was incurring continuous losses over the last three years that had eroded its net worth, how in the absence of any viable

---

[94]'The Lakshmi Vilas Bank Ltd. Placed under Moratorium', Reserve Bank of India, 17 November 2020, https://bit.ly/3GUuIXB. Accessed on 29 November 2022.

strategic plans the losses are expected to continue. It also spoke of how the bank's talks for bringing in additional money had not fructified, which consequently led to the 30-day moratorium.

'The RBI assured the depositors that their money was safe and that soon the bank would be merged with another bank. A year earlier, in September 2019, the central bank had placed LVB under the Prompt Corrective Action, or PCA, framework. Since it had not worked, the RBI ended up upping the ante with a view to protecting depositors' money.

'A deal had been in the making for over a year. In September 2019, the RBI restrained LVB from giving fresh loans. While the LVB promoters were talking with prospective investors, the RBI busied itself with Plan B.

'The regulator had spoken to a few banks in the private sector and two of them, including DBS Bank India Limited (DBIL), had put in their proposals. In the end, DBIL won because its terms were more liberal.

'The central bank penciled an amalgamation scheme of LVB with DBS Bank. Ten days later, on 27 November 2020, the moratorium was lifted, and all LVB branches started operating as branches of DBS Bank India. In addition, the RBI asked LVB to write off around ₹316.80 crore of Tier-II bonds, the entire equity capital was valued at zero and LVB was delisted from the stock exchange. Subsequently, DBS injected ₹2,500 crore as fresh equity.'[95]

'Wow!' said Krishna. 'That was a lightning-speed rescue.'

'Yes, very true, but there were disturbing questions being asked too.' It was Junior.

---

[95]Merwin, Radhika, 'RBI Writes Down LVB Tier 2 Bonds: What Are These Bonds and Why Have Investors Been Caught Unawares?' *The Hindu BusinessLine*, 27 November 2020, https://bit.ly/3VF4cpj. Accessed on 29 November 2022; Mohan, Ashwin, 'LVB-DBS Deal: Post Equity Capital, RBI Directs LVB to Write off Tier-2 Bonds As Well', MoneyControl, 27 November 2020, https://bit.ly/3gDejfu. Accessed on 29 November 2022; 'DBS Bank India Gets ₹2,500 Crore Capital Support from Parent for LVB Merger', *The Times of India*, 4 December 2020, https://bit.ly/3XKmpDt. Accessed on 29 November 2022.

'Like what?' asked Krishna.

'The alacrity with which a suitor was brought in and how the terms and conditions clearly violated the interest of the bondholders and the equity shareholders.'

'What do you mean by that?'

'For instance, the value of both bond and equity was set at zero. It is impossible to believe that the value of a firm that had been in business for 94 years and which had branches across India would have zero value. At least the brand would have commanded a value. I don't know who had valued the bank at zero.'

'Was the matter never investigated?'

'I wouldn't know.'

'There were 560-odd branches and 1.75 million retail customers with the bulk of the bad loans provided for. DBIL would also get the income tax benefit for absorbing ₹2,901 crore of LVB's past losses. It could not be sweeter than that for DBIL.'

'What do you think could have saved LVB?'

Senior was the man with an encyclopaedic knowledge, so he took over. 'Well, for one, LVB could have stuck to its knitting. As long as it focussed on being a local bank, it was fine, but it wished to become corporate without setting up the proper infrastructure for it. It chased corporate clients, forsaking its original mandate of meeting the needs and requirements of local traders. As a result, a quarter of its loan book went bad.'

'What do you mean?' continued Krishna.

'Let me tell you a story. Once, someone set up a ramshackle eatery outside a college campus. It had worn-out furniture and was ill maintained. But the boys and girls loved it because it gave them a homely feeling. As customers poured in, money came in large doses. Soon, the owner refurbished the place. In another six months' time, he had more money, and so he air-conditioned the restaurant. Gradually, the crowd stopped coming.'

'Oh! Why?' It was Krishna.

'Because, with it now air-conditioned and well-maintained,

it was like any other restaurant and lost its unique selling proposition, or what we commonly call USP. In India, the historic practice is not to let banks fail. There is an automatic insurance cover for a set amount. The clever way is to split your money across banks without exceeding that limit,' explained Senior. 'This is how the government protects investors.'

'Smart! But has any bank been allowed to fail so far?'

'None since the liberalization of 1991, although a few cooperative banks have crashed. Each time there was a threat, the RBI stepped in and found a PSU bank to take over.'

'So, what would be the lessons from the LVB deal?' Krishna wondered aloud.

'One, the public sector bank is no longer being used as a vehicle to protect the depositors of sick private banks. Two, foreign banks will now seek local incorporation to take over failing banks. Three, the deal tells promoters that you must shape up, or you ship out.'

Junior, who had just completed a course on behavioural finance, said, 'LVB suffered from the Icarus paradox.'

Krishna groaned. 'Stop showing off! And tell me what that means.'

'Icarus is a figure from Greek mythology. He created wings out of feathers and bees' wax to escape an island. But enamoured by his new-found ability to fly, he ignored warnings not to fly too close to the sun. Upon getting close to the sun, the beeswax melted, his wings fell off and Icarus plummeted to his death.

'Ever since, the term "Icarus paradox" refers to a situation where businesses fail after a period of success. Honchos can be led up the garden path if they fail to predict the outcomes of risky projects. Decisions based on mindless optimism can lead to long-term setbacks. LVB, here, is a case in point.'

LAKSHMI'S NIVAS GONE

When the ceremonial rites of the once-celebrated South-headquartered institution were performed, it had 566 branches and over 4,000 employees, and did business in 19 states and one union territory.[96] Truth be told, it should never have come to such a situation. The bank collapsed on 17 November 2020 and merged with DBS 11 days later, on 27 November.

The story begins in 1926, when seven businessmen led by V.S.N. Ramalinga Chettiar set up a bank to support small businesses in and around Karur. Called Lakshmi Vilas after the Goddess of Wealth, the bank kept up a reasonable pace with time: mechanizing administration in 1977, starting off computerization in 1993 and implementing the Core Banking Solution in 2006. Then, in 2009, it decided to embark on a growth strategy that would shift customer focus from small and medium enterprises (SMEs) to corporate giants. As subsequent events showed, it was the perfect recipe for disaster.

Crisis

LVB had deposits of ₹20,973 crore. A fourth of the bank's advance had turned turtle. Its Gross NPA stood at 25.4 per cent as of June 2020. Only three years earlier, in March 2017, the bad loans were a mere 2.7 per cent; they rose to 10 per cent in 2018, to 15.3 per cent in 2019 and 25.4 per cent in 2020. LVB's Tier-I CAR turned negative as of 30 June 2020, with it posting losses for 10 straight quarters. In September 2020, the shareholders booted out seven members from the board.[97]

So, what went wrong in the nearly 100-year-old bank? One reason was the strategic shift from retail loans towards corporate loans. In

---

[96]'566 New Branches, 4,000 Employees: What Will DBS Bank Get from Lakshmi Vilas Bank?' *Business Today*, 18 November 2020, https://bit.ly/3il1YwK. Accessed on 29 November 2022.

[97]'Lakshmi Vilas Bank Has Enough Liquidity to Pay Back Depositors: RBI-Appointed Official', *Outlook*, 18 November 2022, https://bit.ly/3EKxBaM. Accessed on 29 November 2022; Matthew, George, and Sunny Verma, 'Moratorium on Lakshmi Vilas Bank: What Does It Mean for Depositors, Financial Sector?' *The Indian Express*, 26 November 2020, https://bit.ly/3VfRZrd. Accessed on 29 November 2022.

2008–09, the bank stepped up the ante in a bid to grow. It took positions in infrastructure, textiles and metal, and participated in big-ticket consortiums.

Corporate lending is a two-edged sword. On the one hand, it shores up advances and given the size, the absolute amount of earning is significant. The numbers speak for themselves. The bank's loan book was continuously on the rise. Between March 2007 and March 2010, it rose from ₹3,612 crore to ₹6,277 crore. By March 2013, it touched ₹11,702 crore.[98] The bank was getting into infrastructure, pharma, NBFCs, food and beverage, textiles, engineering and cement, to name a few. And the loan amount rose to ₹16,352 crore in March 2015 and ₹25,768 crore in March 2018.[99] But on the other hand, in case of a slide, the consequences were very expensive. They struck the SMEs hard, and that in turn, hit LVB. The loan book—the total value of the loan—began to shrink, which meant that even if the NPA were stagnant in absolute terms, it would increase in percentage terms as the denominator was on a free fall.

The economy began to fall apart, and the biggies—the bigger corporations LVS had lent to—defaulted. This was the exact same problem as with Yes Bank. Once the tsunami of bad loans hit it, it began to flounder. The bank's low NPA had given it an illusory feeling of safety. That was now gone, and fear gripped the bank.

The trouble all along was that LVB lacked the skill set to identify and evaluate large credit proposals. Training the officers on this wasn't easy. And those with experience, who were hired laterally to handle this, did not understand the organization culture at LVB. And so, credit was granted to outfits like Jet Airways, Religare, Café Coffee Day, and the likes.

LVB had loaned close to ₹5,000 crore to companies in the textiles, infrastructure and metals space. These businesses defaulted on their interest payment obligations. The bank wasn't geared to spot the early warning signals.

---

[98] Adhikari, Anand, 'Lakshmi Vilas Bank: The Tale of 5 CEOs and 94-Year Old Lender's Struggle with Bad Loans', *Business Today*, 20 November 2020, https://bit.ly/3jt8EJM. Accessed on 26 December 2022.
[99] Ibid.

When an existing company wants to raise fresh money as equity, it will have to give the existing shareholders the first right to participate in the issue. Only if they refuse can it be offered to others. Since the shareholders have the first right of refusal, it is called rights issue. In the third quarter of 2017, LVS went for a rights issue and was opaque about its finances. The rights issue involved a fat premium of ₹112 against a face value of ₹10. Post the issue, the third quarter came, and the bank showed a loss of ₹39 crores besides a rise in NPAs. The share prices crashed to ₹12. The shareholders weren't amused and lodged a complaint with SEBI about non-disclosure of material facts in the prospectus.

Some of the consortium loans ended up in the insolvency courts, and the bank had to take huge hits to its profit and loss accounts. One such loan became the proximate cause for the crisis and brought things centre stage. This was a loan of ₹791 crore given to the Singh brothers, Malvinder and Shivinder, the former promoters of Ranbaxy and Religare Healthcare (now Fortis Healthcare). The bank believed that these were secured against fixed deposits of ₹791 crore of the two companies.[100] When the brothers defaulted, LVB appropriated the fixed deposit. Religare Finvest, the new owners of the two companies, sued LVB, saying they had never collateralized the deposit. Legally, they were right, though the case is still pending before the Delhi High Court.[101]

Post the Religare scare, the RBI put LVB under PCA due to the high incidence of bad loans, inability to meet CAR norms and a negative return on assets for two years. The PCA move meant the bank was restrained from making further advances and asked to focus on recoveries from the existing loan book. However, LVB was left high and dry.

LVB began its search for a buyer that would infuse cash into the system and so rescue it. The first option was Indiabulls Housing Finance

[100]'Religare: Singh Brothers, Few Lakshmi Vilas Bank Staff Chargesheeted in ₹791 Crore Fraud', Money Life, 16 April 2020, https://bit.ly/3gJOuu1. Accessed on 29 November 2022.
[101]'Adjustment of Religare Finvest's over ₹790 Cr Deposits Legal: Lakshmi Vilas Bank', The Times of India, 12 June 2018, https://bit.ly/3UhoWCr. Accessed on 29 November 2022.

(IBHF). But then, the RBI refused to give permission to talk to IBHF for money after reports revealed that IBHF might have its own bad loan problems. LVB then turned to Clix Capital, but that, too, fell through as the private equity, after showing initial interest, backed out due to valuation issues. The fund wanted the bank to provide for the contingent liability of ₹791 crore related to Religare Finvest, meaning they wanted the bank to debit the profit and loss account with this amount. Such provisioning would lower the bank's valuation, and LVB wasn't willing to accommodate this request. The case is still ongoing.[102]

Governance Deficit

Along with the poor judgement exercised in giving out loans, LVB was also guilty of banking malpractices. These were also instrumental in ultimately leading to its downfall. For example, some of the directors interfered in the daily working of the bank. Slowly, the asset quality in the bank declined.

In 2012, the RBI highlighted that LVB had conducted transactions with the promoter that was good corporate governance practice. The bank had leased premises from one of its directors without verifying comparable rent. The RBI expressed concerns about data integrity and the lack of a reliable management information system. And it was quite unhappy with how the bank did not strictly adhere to Know Your Customer (KYC) and Anti-Money Laundering norms. Further, there was a corporate governance deficit in LVB.

All these issues combined to result in the bank's downfall and its subsequent absorption into DBS. The lesson here is clear: even a 90-year-old institution, which had done so well for itself, could collapse due to poor decision-making and strategy.

In a later-day development, the Supreme Court allowed minority shareholders' requests to transfer all cases involving the bank's merger with DBS Bank of India to the Madras High Court.

---

[102]*Religare Finvest Limited vs Lakshmi Vilas Bank Limited on 29 March, 2022*, India Kanoon, https://bit.ly/3iaokRt. Accessed on 29 November 2022.

19

KRISHNA BEGINS HIS DRAFT

With every discussion, Krishna had been taking copious notes in his notepad. His idea was to develop a comprehensive piece for his school magazine. And he wanted it to look professional. He even marked out the areas that needed more study and investigation.

Years ago, his mother had won an award in her school for writing, and she had been proud of it. Today, as he read through the prize-winning piece, it brought tears to his eyes. It reminded him of her.

He began to write.

The first banking infraction in independent India was in 1957, when the government asked LIC to invest in six companies in which rogue trader Haridas Mundhra had a stake. The corporation lost money, and Feroze Gandhi, **(Note to self: write about what he looks like)** kicked up a shindy. A commission passed strictures on the Congress party; Chacha Nehru snubbed the judge and later apologized for it.

In the middle of 1971, Jimmy Nagarwala, a former intelligence agent, walked away with ₹60 lakh from an SBI branch imitating the voice of Mrs Gandhi. He was caught the same day, tried expeditiously, and the cop who handled his case died in a road accident. In prison, Jimmy was felled by a heart attack on his fifty-first birthday. The full story will never be known.

After India opened up its economy in 1991, Harshad Mehta, a former insurance clerk, understood the shortcomings of the bond market and conned bankers with his smooth talk and deep knowledge. It was a classic case of teeming and lading. (**Note to self: Explain this phrase**). Mehta died while in prison. Like the FBI, who released Frank Abagnale to help nab criminals, maybe the SEBI could have used Mehta to tighten up the law.

Mehta's protégé, Ketan Parekh, carried his legacy forward, and in early 2000 used circuit trading, pumping and dumping (**Note to self: must explain these terms**) to rig up shares. He brought the Global Trust Bank to its knees in the process.

The King of Good Times, Vijay Mallya, who ran Kingfisher booze with elan, met his Waterloo in Kingfisher Airlines. It destroyed him comprehensively after he ran huge debts with banks. It was never clear why the banks didn't agree to his one-time settlement offers, while in many other cases, they did. Was it a political decision? (**Note to self: must explain these and give my views on it while writing the essay**).

Anil Ambani was sixth on the Forbes list but is bankrupt today.

Nirav Modi did to the PNB roughly what Mehta had done to SBI. How he manipulated insiders to give him LoUs without routing through the banking system, and how it did not get caught in inter-branch reconciliation are intriguing stories in themselves.

Both DHFL and IL&FS were outlandish frauds done by greedy promoters and the top brass. They were nothing short of placing one's hand in the till and taking the money away.

How to say 'No' is something Yes Bank never learnt. The result: the promoters ran India's fourth-largest bank to the ground until the regulator stepped in, at the twelfth hour, with a rescue act. State-owned institutions pumped investor money to save the rogue bank.

LVB lost because of overarching ambition. After all, if you have to move from lending to small traders to lending to large corporates, you need a change of perspective. The owners didn't invest enough to make the change. The result: they ground a 94-year-old bank to dust.

PMC Bank represents everything that's wrong with cooperative banks. Political patronage and dubious deals were struck. **(Note to self: Take only five of these 11 cases for writing elucidation in the essay!).**

He ended by putting down in bold red colours a note for himself: **In subsequent sittings, Junior and I should ask GGP about what those who were mandated to guard the bankers did: the auditors, the RBI, the credit rating agencies and the directors.**

PART THREE

SLEEPING AT THE WHEEL?

20

WHERE WERE THE AUDITORS?

They were all supposed to be the cops, or chowkidars, or gatekeepers. Alas, they—the auditors, bank regulators, credit raters and directors—in some way or the other—failed us.

When a company collapses under the weight of fraud, the first question that pops up in the public mind is, 'What were the auditors doing?' Ask a CA, and he will tell you that an external auditor is supposed to be a watchdog and not a bloodhound. He is not expected to track carefully crafted frauds, and his role is restricted to reporting on the truth and fairness of the accounts rather than going sniffing for frauds. Unfortunately, the public is unwilling to buy this argument and thinks that the men-in-suits are often in cohort with the management. That's at least how it is in the twenty-first century.

Could the Harshad Mehta or the Nirav Modi scandal have happened without insiders in the bank working in tandem with the scamster? Or, for that matter, could the extraordinary story of Vijay Mallya have panned out without internal help? Were bankers wet behind the ears, or did they do what they did only in the best interests of their organization? Was there a personal stake in it for them? Even if it was a case of one deal gone wrong that needed hiding and then turned into an avalanche, can they be excused? In short, what has been the role of bankers and of the RBI in the Great Bank Robbery?

Auditors and bankers are not the only ones who come under fire, though. What is the role of credit rating agencies? Aren't these high priests of corporate analysis supposed to help investors make an investment choice? But the agencies have also been blind to the dark acts of companies—they couldn't see them shrink, and didn't give investors adequate time to get out. There have also been charges of rating shopping on the rise.

Finally, come the bank directors. They are meant to be guardians of corporate governance and are expected to stand up to promoters' tantrums. They are the company's trustees and are there to mentor the management. Some of these directors are independent under the law, meaning they are not beholden to promoters. These are men with rich corporate experience; others have been in academia and done extensive research. But boards in companies have not kept a very tight vigil. That, at least, is the charge. Did these men, as the company's gatekeepers, fail in their job? Or, was it that they were too busy to fulfill their role?

◆

Lobin Stephen Junior had jotted down the above points for a speech he was to deliver when classes resumed at Harvard after the holidays. He knew this was as of now only half done, but after he and Krishna had a few more sessions with their GGP, he would have enough material for his 18-minute talk.

It was 7.30 p.m. The three continued with their conversation at the lawn of the Stephens' sprawling house, post-dinner.

'GGP, we have talked about so many cases of fraud now. But how did all this happen when there were people to oversee the system? Like when there were auditors, board members, credit raters and the regulators?' wondered Junior aloud.

Senior said, 'Often, those who should be in the know are the last ones to know.'

'What do you mean?' Krishna asked.

'For example, if Junior is going steady with someone, the whole world gets to know about it before his mom does.' Senior laughed at his own joke.

Krishna ignored the comment and said, 'GGP, you cannot be serious. Their job is to know.'

'Maybe. Maybe not. The reality is that they turn out to be the last ones to get a sniff of the crisis. And there are reasons for it. To understand their position, you should understand their job.'

'Okay, let's start with the auditor. What is his job?'

Junior stepped in. 'You see, different types of auditors audit banks and companies. In banks, you have the RBI auditors, the concurrent auditors and the statutory auditors. In companies, you have internal auditors and external auditors.'

Krishna asked, 'So, what is an RBI audit?'

'Good question. The RBI inspects a bank's account books to verify that they follow the rules. It investigates credit, market and operational risk, and assesses the bank's possibility of failure.

'RBI officials look at the position of the various loans, the NPAs and the reasons for the NPAs. They probe the irregularities during the sanctioning process. The report is then discussed with the bank head and later presented to the RBI's board of financial supervision headed by the governor.' It was Senior.

'With so many checks, they should spot the crisis early.'

'Yes, they should have picked warning signals. Maybe they did even.'

'What do you mean by that last part?' asked Junior.

'Well, take the case of a football match. You celebrate players who score goals. You don't measure them by how many they missed. Yet, you judge a goalkeeper by the number of goals conceded, not by the ones he saved. Auditors are like goalkeepers.'

'You mean there are several times when audits have spotted frauds, but these have not come in the public domain because there is nothing sensational about it. Right?'

'You nailed it, Junior.'

Krishna jumped in. 'Can you tell me what other kinds of audits take place?'

'Concurrent audit,' replied Junior. 'Legal audit. Stock audit.

Revenue audit. Statutory audit. Before you ask, let me explain each one.' Junior got into the all-knowing elder-brother mood. 'A bank needs its financial transactions to be audited on the fly. For example, when you purchase some notebooks, you must show the bills to me immediately.'

Krishna winced. 'You mean I must show you proof of my spending?'

'Chill! This is the essence of concurrent audit. It is intended to provide timely detection of irregularities.

'Then, there is legal audit, wherein title deeds are re-verified. This verification is essential as banks advance funds against collaterals. Stock audits involve inspecting assets pledged with the bank and used by borrowers. Revenue audit is about verifying the accuracy of incomes earned and ensuring no leakage. And finally, statutory audit is where external auditors look into the books to express a view on the truth and fairness of accounts.'

'Phew! I am sure you haven't missed any.'

'I have. I skipped Information Technology (IT) audit.'

'Audits, audits, everywhere, but not a fraud to spot,' sang Krishna.

'That's unfair,' said Junior. 'It is not that auditors have always napped, or not taken responsibility. Deloitte resigned from DHFL citing a lack of sufficient evidence to form an opinion on the financial statement of the company. Earlier, they had filed a fraud complaint with the corporate affairs ministry. In fact, the statutory auditors pointed to transactions of ₹40,000 crore that were troublesome.[103]

'Deloitte also flagged concerns in Nirav Modi's Firestar International Ltd, stating that the company did not have an

---

[103]Upadhyay, Jayshree P., 'DHFL Auditors Filed a Fraud Complaint with MCA in August', mint, 6 November 2019, https://bit.ly/3FbIpjB. Accessed on 29 November 2022; Rajput, Rashmi, 'Probe Former DHFL Brass for Causing ₹40,000 Crore Loss to Lenders: Union Bank to CBI', The Economic Times, 30 November 2021, https://bit.ly/3ARJuKA. Accessed on 29 November 2022.

"appropriate internal control system".[104] Ernst & Young had pointed to the possibility of "rogue" employees in PNB.'

'So, tell me how the scam was not spotted for so long,' asked Krishna.

'Let me give you the example of PNB. The process was foolproof. At Brady House, the branch manager is an assistant general manager, and a senior executive works as a "concurrent auditor". The latter's job is to audit the day's transactions and by 5 p.m., to generate an audit report co-signed by the manager. The auditor reports directly to headquarters and is not answerable to anyone in the branch.' Junior was clearly on a roll explaining things to his younger cousin with aplomb.

'So far so good. But what happened was a few LoUs were issued, and these did not go through the bank's core banking system. Hence, the concurrent auditor wasn't equipped to figure it out.

'The statutory auditors possibly did not find it out, because their work is at a macro level, and they rely on internal audit reports. Additionally, the audit performed by the RBI does not necessarily look into daily operations.'

Krishna was annoyed. 'In short, you are saying, no one can be faulted for not figuring it out, and yet, there is a huge amount paid as audit fees?'

Junior was at his explaining best, much to the surprise of Senior. 'Well, the internal auditors should have cracked it. In the case of PNB, even if SWIFT and CBS did not talk to each other, the transaction went into the nostro account overseas. SWIFT is a messaging network that financial institutions use to securely transmit information and instructions through a standardized system of codes. CBS, or Core Banking Solution, is the networking of bank branches, which allows customers to

[104]Narayan, Khushboo, 'PNB Fraud: Auditor Deloitte Rang Alarm Bells on Nirav Modi Two Years Ago', *The Indian Express*, 18 February 2018, https://bit.ly/3gNlKkg. Accessed on 29 November 2022.

manage their accounts, and use various banking facilities from any part of the world.

'An audit of the foreign branch should have easily picked it up. But perhaps because it is a specialized function, and because internal auditors are experts at accounts and not in forex, they must have missed it.

'It's important to understand that auditors will not be able to spot a fraud unless they are looking for one. And it becomes impossible for them to do this if the people within the organization cooperate with the fraudsters. Read GGP's piece titled "Every Fraud Has Gone Through an Audit".'

They all agreed to meet three days later.

EVERY FRAUD HAS GONE THROUGH AN AUDIT

Right or wrong, the high-profile nature of frauds throws the auditor open to the charge that he in some manner contributed to the fraud. While no one has pointed the needle of suspicion directly at him, enough and more hints have been thrown that he was either foxed by the fraudster, or worse still, was negligent.

The Landmark Judgment

In 1896, came the judgment in the Kingston Cotton Mills case in England. Lord Justice Lopes ruled,

> It is the duty of an auditor to bring to bear on the work he has to perform that skill, care, and caution which a reasonably careful, cautious auditor would use. What is a reasonable skill, care, and caution must depend on the particular circumstances of each case? He is a watchdog, not a bloodhound. He is justified in believing tried servants of the company in whom confidence is placed by the company. He is entitled to assume that they

are honest and rely upon their representations, provided he takes reasonable care.[105]

This judgment served to define the role of an auditor and has been frequently quoted since, especially in response to accusations against auditors.

Enron, WorldCom, Tyco[106] and Xerox abroad, and Satyam, IL&FS and DHFL in India have shown that accounting frauds occur frequently and cause great damage to the economy at large. And the role of auditors was increasingly coming into the open. In Satyam, the ICAI suspended two auditors of Price Waterhouse S. Gopalakrishnan and Srinivas Talluri, for life, even though one of them pointed out that it was impossible to detect carefully crafted frauds. This is especially difficult when your job is not hunting for frauds, but commenting only on the truth and fairness of accounts.

In the case of some of the scandals that we have covered, the audit report in the immediate previous year was as white as snow, even as data subsequently suggested that they ought to have been as black as coal.

Knowledge of Business

Harshad Mehta's was a case of teeming and lading. Auditors of that period were not precisely very conversant with how the bond market worked, and you really could not fault them for not spotting it. Ketan Parekh pumped the market, and the auditors could possibly do very little about what lay squarely within the bandwidth of the regulators. We are not sure if the external auditors are called upon to judge the propriety of an advance. Auditors are only required to state whether a payment was for business purpose, was authorized, was expended and if there is evidence for it. For example, commenting on whether I should have three mobiles or 10 is not the auditor's job. They could not comment on pumping the market.

---

[105]Gandhi, Ruchi, 'A Summary of Kingston Cotton Mills Case', Finlawportal, 2 September 2022, https://bit.ly/3UKWDwy. Accessed on 10 November 2022.
[106]One of the authors, Sabyasachee Dash, worked in the tax function of Tyco group in India between 2014 and 2017.

The trouble with the PNB case involving Nirav Modi was that the transactions took place outside the books. But there was enough material in the books that, just maybe, the auditors could have spotted. But the problem is that auditors are often required to work at breakneck speed and use templates for auditing, so it is natural that many of the more subtle indicators get missed. And in the case of PMC, the auditors acted perhaps in good faith, looking only at fresh advances. This can explain what happened, even if it doesn't expunge them of any responsibility.

Auditors Hauled, But...

Auditors were indeed held responsible for their role in letting such fraud happen. In 2021, NFRA held two auditors of IL&FS guilty of professional misconduct. The NFRA concluded that the IL&FS auditor compromised on his independence by rendering non-audit services to group companies at high fees and that the engagement partner did not involve himself fully in the audit. Also, while default on one instalment brought the IL&FS down, the statutory auditors had said nothing about the idea of a 'going concern' being in doubt. 'Going concern' is an accounting term for a company that has the resources needed to continue operating indefinitely. It also refers to an organization's ability to make enough money to avoid bankruptcy. If an entity is not a going concern, it means it's going bankrupt.

Regulators in India and across the globe have tried several tricks to set things right. Rotation of auditors, under which the auditor changes after a given number of years, is one such measure. Mandating joint audits, where more than one auditor audits a company, is another. Prohibition of specified non-audit service was a third.

The audit report in 2022 is a massive volume. The extent of the report depends on the nature and extent of the company's operations, the various regulators to which it is answerable and runs often into hundreds of pages giving a plethora of information.

Unfortunately, it is the same management that appoints the

auditors which pays them. In short, the one who appoints and pays is the same over whose work the auditor is to audit. There has to be some mechanism, at least in the case of listed companies, to start with where a central agency selects the auditor and pays out the fees after collecting it from the pool of companies.

An element of scepticism has become a default factor during the business performance evaluation. The more robust the governance mechanism, the better is the reliance quotient reposed in the management. In this context, the role of independent auditors and directors becomes vital. While the auditor plays the role of a watchdog, the independent director acts as a trustee for the shareholders. Both parties challenge the management, while the independent directors are additionally responsible for governance-related matters. While this looks simple on paper, its execution is not easy.[107]

Threats and Safeguards

According to the International Federation of Accountants, there are five threats to an auditor's independence: self-interest threats, self-review threats, advocacy threats, familiarity threats and intimidation threats, which are unfortunately not easy to safeguard against.

For the public to have confidence in audit quality, auditors must be independent of the entities being audited. The auditor should possess integrity, objectivity and professional scepticism, which are prerequisites to independence. Before taking on any work, he must conscientiously consider whether it would involve threats to his freedom. If he finds any, he should either desist from the task or, at the very least, put in place safeguards that would eliminate those threats.

To improve the quality of reporting, we must free the auditor from the intimidation of being fired and put in place measures to eradicate the risk of a conflict of interest. Laying down a process to ensure the appointment of auditors by an independent agency other than the

---

[107]Chopra, Amarjit, and Sabyasachee Dash, 'Improving Audit Quality: Significance of Independence and Capacity Building', *ICAI Journal*, 1 June 2021, pp. 59–62.

management, at least in the case of public interest entities, is a key to providing independence to auditors.

Joint audits are being contemplated. Public-spirited organizations are suggesting that companies of a certain size and scale should have joint audits and it has even been adopted by some IT majors known for sound corporate governance. While there is no proof to suggest that having more than one audit firm jointly perform the audit of a company is more efficient than an individual audit, it is believed that it could allow discussions and consequently better results. History shows that a joint audit has worked very well in the audit of public sector banks and PSUs.

The need to reduce the concentration in a few hands of audits is well recognized. Monopolies, in any sector, jeopardize the quality of the work. Tenders floated by the departments of the government and various entities should not be tailor-made and skewed heavily in favour of certain firms alone. This hampers the development of several Indian firms in the long run.

21

HOW INDEPENDENT ARE INDEPENDENT DIRECTORS?

'I will tell you a story, and then if you are game for another, I will tell you the second one,' said Senior as he settled on his easy chair and began to smoke his pipe.

'Go ahead, go ahead,' said an excited Krishna. He loved stories, and had even thought of taking up storytelling as a career.

Senior said, 'I will not name the bank, and so do not pester me for it.'

Krishna turned towards his cousin and snorted, 'I think GGP worked in those banks.' Seeing Senior's face turn a shade of red, he didn't continue with what he thought was a good joke.

'Go ahead, GGP. Ignore Brat,' remarked Junior.

'Years ago, the central bank did not share bank inspection reports with the public. A public-spirited analyst used the Right to Information Act, or RTI Act, and the courts to get the bank to share these reports. The report painted a picture which was quite different from what the bank painted of itself in its annual report.'

A streak of pain crossed Senior's face as he remembered what the banks and companies had done. 'The annual report is addressed to the shareholders. The management owes its job to these shareholders and cannot be economical with the truth. You must read any one of Warren Buffett's several letter to shareholders to understand what is being transparent and candid.'

Krishna wanted the conversation back on the bank. He said, 'Agreed, GGP. What did this bank do?'

'The bank was poorly governed. Its board had subcommittees

for IT strategy, risk management and human resources (HR). These committees barely did any work. For instance, the IT committee would meet without an IT expert attending. The HR committee never met for two whole years, even when the bank had trouble recruiting people. Finally, there were practically no risk mitigation plans in place.

'The board did not have a clear policy on the appointment of directors to overseas bodies. There was no adequate role description for people who were deputed from some of these affiliates and subsidiaries.'

'How can that be?' asked Junior.

'I wouldn't know. There are worse examples. A board directive said that the zones underperforming on loan recovery should make a presentation at each board meeting. But it was ignored. And the board chairman as well as the audit committee ignored this lapse.

'Some of the findings raised integrity issues. Thanks to a software bug, the risk-weighted assets were under-counted and helped the bank to tide over capital-adequacy requirements. The capital adequacy ratio, or CAR, is a measure of how much capital a bank has available, as a percentage of a bank's risk-weighted assets. The objective is to check if those banks have enough capital to handle a certain amount of losses, before being at risk of becoming insolvent. The higher a bank's CAR, the more likely it is that it will withstand financial shock.'

'That's so convenient,' remarked Junior.

'Worse followed. A large amount was categorized as restructured loans, and soon a good part of it slipped back to the default category.'

'How convenient!'

'Troublesome sectors, such as NBFCs and real estate, were incorrectly classified, thus pushing capital adequacy up. Loans were disbursed to NBFCs for onward lending on the strength of a certificate from a CA. And there was no tracking for these.'

Junior got up, alarmed. This was everything contrary to what he had learnt in corporate governance classes. 'My God! How could this happen?'

Senior gestured him to calm down, saying, 'It just happened. The bank was tardy in referring and pursuing cases under the Securitization and Reconstruction of Financial Assets and Enforcement of Security Interest Act, called the SARFAESI Act, and following up on debt recovery tribunal, or DRT proceedings. The internal audit was inadequate, but the external auditors did not mention it. Several findings of the systems were unreliable, but there were no references to these in the board meetings.'

Junior suddenly had a flash of insight. 'Is this the same bank that paid fines to overseas regulators for compliance failures?'

'That's right,' said Senior.

'What kind of board oversaw these operations?' asked Krishna, a little alarmed.

'Well,' said Junior. 'It had a Harvard MBA, an IIM don and a former Big-Four partner.' He winked at his GGP, indicating he knew the name of the bank.

Senior nodded.

◆

When they met again in the evening, Krishna said to Senior, 'You promised us a second story.'

'Yes, I did indeed. What happened was this. In the case of another bank, the RBI questioned its functioning in areas of risk management, IT security, HR and digital banking. Surprisingly, it was in these very areas that the bank had won a few Golden Peacock Awards.'

'What!' exclaimed Krishna, surprised. 'How does one get awards for lapses, inefficiencies and noncompliance?'

'I told you; this kind of thing happens. Worse still, over 300 internal audit reports piled up awaiting disposal. By the way, the RBI inspectors slammed the management for not adhering to the risk management policy, not having a succession plan for critical positions, not looking into IT security and ballooning of bad loans.

'IT security was compromised. The board seemed to turn a blind eye to overseas operations, and the bank was found averse to recruiting a senior personnel and to carrying out staff rotation.

'I was informed by a senior analyst that the board did not lay out proper policies for asset and liability management. This important step in the banking business was skipped and, as a result, the bank was juggling liquidity with 14-day deposits!'

Krishna asked, 'What did the statutory auditors say?'

Junior stepped in. He again seemed to know the identity of the bank. 'Six firms from different parts of India, in their considered professional wisdom, gave a clean report.'

'But what were the directors doing?' Krishna asked.

'They attended the meetings. If they knew of the problems and stayed on, they were guilty of abetment. If they didn't think they were guilty, they were staying there as puppets.'

'The moral,' said Krishna, 'is that the RBI auditors did their jobs, and you cannot brush them aside with one sweeping stroke.'

Senior looked sharply at Krishna. With the specs resting at the end of his nose, he asked, 'What! Are you planning to study chartered accountancy? You seem to be siding with the RBI inspectors?'

Junior had the last word. 'GGP, by the time we finish, Brat will have at various points dreamed of becoming an auditor, a banker, a credit rater, a director or a super cop.'

Krishna felt it was best to ignore the jibe, so he smiled sweetly and went off, clutching his precious notepad.

Meanwhile, the boys knew that sometime today, GGP would send them a mail to be read. They weren't wrong.

WHAT IT TAKES TO BE DIRECTOR

The economic reforms initiated in India in 1991 gave birth to a new era in corporate governance. In 1992, SEBI ushered in capital market reforms. In 1999, a committee chaired by Kumar Mangalam Birla urged market regulator SEBI to promote the standard of corporate governance for listed companies. This led to the drafting of the Equity Listing Agreement. This was the origin of concepts such as an independent board and audit committee.

Shareholders have high expectations from independent directors, but at times, these are misplaced, as various scams and cases of fraud occurring over the last several years show.

But remember: an individual independent director cannot act in isolation. He can, at best, initiate a discussion. He alone cannot stop a decision, and neither can he turn into a whistleblower, because board meetings are confidential. In certain companies, banks and PSUs, the nominee directors have been found wanting in their job.

The only way independent directors can stop wrong choices is by banding together. Even then, they cannot be expected to prevent 'management fraud', as turning the independent directors into policemen in the boardroom will be detrimental to the managers' freedom of enterprise. By discharging its responsibility of ensuring effective internal control, the board must depend on institutions such as internal audit, external audit and legal counsel. Therefore, the effectiveness of independent directors depends on the independence and effectiveness of those institutions.

In January 2019, precisely 10 years after the Satyam scandal broke out, another corporate fraud became sensational: DHFL. Like the Satyam scandal, the fraudsters were the promoters. These companies had the same email IDs and the same group of initial directors.

The moot point is whether there is sufficient evidence to prove that the directors in the Satyam scam or the DHFL case were hand in glove with the perpetrators or whether merely being on the board would mean that their assets could be seized. Seizure would be fair only if it was proven that the IDs connived in the wrongdoing and personally gained from it.

For sure, after this, these directors will walk the extra mile to raise any red flags. However, they don't spend a lot of time in the company, and to penalize them this way will not serve any purpose.

The lesson is that independent directors must ensure adequate internal checks and controls are put in place, and there is secure risk management and balanced decision-making. These directors work based on the information they get from the management and can therefore offer views only regarding matters that come to their notice. You cannot expect them to act as cops in the boardroom. They will have to be that much more careful and not continue to play yes-men.

◆

In a monarchy, there is the state, the king and his subjects, and the three interact in clearly defined ways. Now substitute the state with the corporation; the king with the board, and the subjects with various stakeholders, and you have the basics of corporate governance. At its heart is the belief that public good should come ahead of private greed.

Kautilya's *Arthashastra* spoke about 'good governance'. Good governance and stability are interconnected. If rulers are responsive, accountable and removable, there is stability; otherwise, instability will prevail. He also spoke about *Raksha, Vriddhi, Palana and Yogakshema*— all of these hold even today. 'Raksha' means protection. In the corporate world, it means risk management. 'Vriddhi' means growth. Today, it refers to stakeholder value enhancement. 'Palana' means compliance. This is the modern equivalent of adherence to the law. 'Yogakshema' implies the social security system. In the corporate context, it can be equated to corporate social responsibility.[108]

A good corporate entity makes decisions that consider economic,

---

[108]'Shaving the Barber I', *The Statesman*, Kolkata, 12 February 2021.

social and regulatory compliance. The directors must align the interests of the board, management and shareholders, and must provide oversight, insight and foresight. In every decision, the board must ponder its effects on employees, customers, suppliers, communities and shareholders. Needless to say, the role of the directors is different from that of managers.

The board represents the interest of promoters, the CEO, senior executives, prominent investors, and in some cases, workers and financial institutions. Each director must place the company's interests above everything else, but this may not always happen. This creates the need for independent directors.

The directors are responsible for strategic planning and oversight. The board takes the opinions of external experts to assist them in case they feel necessary. In their role as overseers, the board must continually assess risks in financial reporting, internal controls, reputation, environment, ethics, health and safety. They are not there to micromanage the management.

Globally, the five virtues expected of independent directors are impartiality, availability, expertise, resolution of conflicts and expansion of network. Ideally, the antennae of independent directors should go up whenever they see a related party transaction. To be honest about their jobs, the independent directors must exercise their independent professional judgement in decision-making and be brave about voicing their views in the boardroom.

Mervyn King wrote, 'Good corporate governance is about "intellectual honesty" and not just sticking to rules and regulations, capital flowed towards companies that practiced this type of good governance.'[109]

According to the law, these men can be paid up to ₹1 lakh as sitting fees per board meeting. Companies can pay more as a commission on profits. The total commission paid to all non-executive directors, including independent directors, in a company can be as much as 1 per

---

[109]'Thoughts on Corporate Governance', India's 100 Richest, *Forbes India*, 11 July 2015, https://bit.ly/3gKHvky. Accessed on 30 November 2022.

cent of its profit. As per reports, the number of independent directors taking home over ₹1 crore annually is rising.[110]

It is widely perceived that higher compensation tends to dilute the effectiveness of these men. Simultaneously, without an adequate compensation mechanism, it's impossible to find top-notch talent, thereby creating a Catch-22 situation.

Also, certain bureaucrats and bankers who have handled the companies' files in their official capacity have been accepting board positions in the same companies post-retirement. It may be legally permissible, but is it ethically justified? And, won't this be a fit case of quid pro quo?

In the end, the litmus test for an effective independent director lies in the independence of judgement and absence of a material pecuniary relationship.

From an analyst's perspective, they should look out for red flags. These include accounting anomalies, significant growth when the industry returns a weak performance, multiple related party transactions and off-balance sheet items.

In most cases, what galls many directors is that agencies that conduct investigations paint all members of the board of the company with the same brush. A common complaint is that agencies often fail to distinguish the role of the independent director from those who have an operational role in the company.

The Expert Committee on Company Law, constituted by the Ministry of Corporate Affairs (MCA), had this to say on the role of independent directors: 'Independent directors should be able to bring an element of objectivity to the Board process.'[111]

It is the job of the independent directors to protect the public stake in the company. They can raise red flags only on issues that come

[110]Bhattacharyya, Rica, 'More Independent Directors Earn in Crores Now', *The Economic Times*, 5 December 2019, https://bit.ly/3GSm0ci. Accessed on 30 November 2022.
[111]'Independent Directors: Role, Responsibilities, Effectiveness', (2019) PL (CL) July 75, https://bit.ly/3XGZw3Z. Accessed on 30 November 2022.

to their knowledge in the ordinary course of business and via board processes. The Indian Institute of Corporate Affairs (IICA) now maintains an online databank of existing and eligible independent directors.[112] There is also a proficiency qualification examination for independent directors, mandating a minimum score of 60 per cent for any individual to qualify for an appointment. The MCA also clarified in March 2020 that civil or criminal proceedings should not unnecessarily be initiated against independent directors, unless enough evidence exists to the contrary and, if already created, must be reviewed.

---

[112]Independent   Director's   Databank,   https://bit.ly/3DZ9Yed.   Accessed   on 10 November 2022.

22

WHO WILL RATE THE RATERS?

'How do I know if this is a good investment to make?' asked Krishna.

Junior pushed back the mountain of hair that swept across his forehead and said, 'You see, we must first look at the macroeconomic variables to know if the economy is doing well and if the country, or as in this case, India is a good place to invest. Then we should look at the industry to ascertain...'

'If you don't know, why don't you say so?' Krishna cruelly cut him short.

Junior burst out laughing watching the injured innocence of his cousin, and the ghost of a smile crossed Senior's face. Senior interjected. 'For his age, you should talk to him about how debt instruments are selected. Not stocks.'

'Well, Krishna, because you lack the patience, or better still because you are too young, maybe you can look at the grade the credit rating agencies assign to an instrument. Rating is like your school grade, and expresses levels of safety in connection with the investment. Based on that, you can select what appeals to you.'

Krishna looked into the far corner of the ceiling and said, 'Rating is an expression of opinion regarding an investment. This is laid out in the form of standardized symbols, which tell you whether the investment is very safe or is about to default. In between, there are various other specifications.'

Junior stared at him and asked, 'How did you know?'

'I crammed it up last night.'

'Bloody cramming machine!'

'It's an opinion and not a mathematical certainty. But the idea is formed based on financial analysts who are arguably experts in the subjects. Ratings are important because they help investors in making investment decisions,' continued Krishna.

'Impressive. Very impressive,' said Junior.

'Boss, you tell me, why do we need credit rating? Especially after the mess that it has swept us into,' asked Krishna.

It was a good question, but Junior gave a perfunctory reply. 'See, the rating indicates the extent of safety inherent in an instrument issued by a company. You will not be able to carry out the analysis all by yourself. Sometimes, having an expert to do the job helps.'

Senior stepped in. 'Junior, I think Krishna has a point. Perhaps I will rephrase his question. These agencies never foresaw the fall of companies, although the markets did. The market read it ahead by hammering the instrument's price down and thus increased the effective interest rate to reflect new realities of risk. But I agree with you. We still require a rater to do the initial rating.'

'You have a point there, GGP,' said Junior. 'By the way, would it not be a good idea that rating agencies stick to just rating and do not get down to doing other things like market research, training and risk solutions? After all, audit firms that do statutory audits are barred from having consulting income beyond a certain size.'

There was a 15-second silence till Krishna pierced it with his love for statistics. 'What has been the volume of work done so far?'

Junior googled and read out. 'In the last 10 years, 205 companies were assigned triple-A ratings. In contrast, in the US S&P (Standard and Poor's 500) index gave out the top slot to 10, and Moody's recommended it in the case of 50 instruments.'

'Ha! Did I not tell you? These rating agencies are easy in handing out ratings,' said Krishna, jumping up and down.

'Hold your horses, my boy. Let me complete the reading. Triple-A in India accounts for only 1 per cent of all rated firms, compared with 10 per cent in China. Out of approximately 50,000 ratings, outstanding as of December 2030, nearly three-fourths are in the "non-investment grade" category. In FY30, Indian credit rating agencies downgraded several 5,000 ratings. This suggests that credit rating agencies haven't shied away from assigning lower ratings or downgrading those who pay for the assessment.'

Krishna hung his head like a beaten tiger but could not resist saying, 'We have seven credit rating agencies, and three of them have access to global best practices through tie-ups, and yet they let us down.'

No one had the head or the heart to disagree with the little one. After all, for his age, he did know a lot.

'I am going to read out the concluding part of an old article that I found in the *Journal of Emerging Market Finance*. The article is titled "Has the Global Financial Crisis Changed the Market Response to Credit Ratings? Evidence from an Emerging Market" and is written by Kaveri Krishnan, Sankarshan Basu and Ashok Thampy.[113] It addresses the question that Krishna raised,' Senior said.

Senior then went on to read from his iPad.

> In India, credit rating agencies have been operational for 30 years, but the introduction of bank loan ratings and IPO grading has been a significant development in India's credit rating industry. The efficacy of the rating process is vital for the development of an active corporate bond market. In an underdeveloped debt market, institutional investors are cautious about their exposure to securities, and the quality of rating is crucial to attract investors and help in better price discovery.

'The report analysed the differential market response to credit rating revisions in pre, during and post the Global Financial Crisis period using data from India. By reviewing the stock price reactions to the announcement of long-term rating changes

---

[113]Krishnan, Kaveri, et al., 'Has the Global Financial Crisis Changed the Market Response to Credit Ratings? Evidence from an Emerging Market', *Journal of Emerging Market Finance*, Vol. 19, No. 1, https://bit.ly/3DX6FUy. Accessed on 10 November 2022.

during the period 1996–2015, the researchers found that the stock market reacted less to rating revisions after the crisis. There is evidence of an overall negative market reaction after rating change announcements. This suggests that credit ratings add value to the Indian financial market. The rating revisions contain some information that is publicly unavailable but relevant for security pricing and can be used by the market participants to make informed decisions. However, the magnitude of the adverse reaction is lower in the post-crisis period. This implies that the incremental value addition by rating agencies has reduced after the crisis. The analysis of rating downgrades also indicates that investors have become more sensitive to downgrades within the investment-grade category post-crisis.

'There could be several other factors driving the market behaviour in the post-crisis period. The lower market reaction could be attributed to credit rating agencies providing no incremental information to the market.

'The lower information content of rating changes in the post-crisis period hints that the market's confidence in the rating information has reduced. Regulators across the world are concerned about the value addition of credit ratings. Instead, they have introduced regulations to make credit rating agencies more accountable and to improve the transparency of the rating process in the post-crisis period. These regulations are expected to strengthen the credibility of the credit rating agencies and regain the market's trust in the rating information.

'Greater information disclosure by rating agencies will help market participants gauge the credit risk in these instruments better and help in the development of Indian capital markets,' said Senior.

Junior saw Krishna blink multiple times. He said, 'Don't worry. It's perfectly understandable if you did not make head or tail of it. GGP will forward it to us, and you can read it three or four times until it sinks in.'

Krishna made a face at his cousin, and the trio agreed that they would look at the road ahead for the banking industry in the following week.

EVERYTHING ISN'T ABOVE BOARD

The rating industry has come under attack often for not fulfilling its duties satisfactorily. In several cases, they have woken up after the horse has bolted. This is despite the impressive pedigrees these raters come with.

Take the case of IL&FS. Set up in 1987, it led the nation's infrastructure story during the last decade and raised billions of dollars in debt. In August 2019, it collapsed, sending the investing public scurrying for cover. It defaulted on its loans from banks, mutual funds and provident funds.

There was enough smoke the previous year, in 2018, but the raters either didn't notice it or thought the companies themselves would sniff it out. And then when the fire became a towering inferno, a rating downgrade happened. In one swoop, it fell from being triple-A rated to being called junk. But by then, it was too late.

The raters, wise men in flannel suits, did not foresee the failing fortunes of IL&FS, even as debt in the group rose by 44 per cent over the four years ended March 2018. This failure was proof that it is not enough to focus on past data and trust the management's estimate of the future, but to have market intelligence and surveillance skills. Remember, even till the previous month, July 2019, the credit rating agencies had investment-grade ratings on instruments raised by the IL&FS Group.

This was not an isolated instance. DHFL, Cox & Kings and Altico Capital, to name only a few, defaulted even while their long-term ratings enjoyed investment grade. This has raised concerns over the quality of ratings and the work of the raters.

So Where Did They and We Go Wrong?

India works on the issuer-pays model. This means that if X Ltd wants its rating done by, say, CRISIL, it pays the agency for it. The plus point in this is that X Ltd will permit CRISIL's analysts to access a wardrobe of information and would be keen to offer regular updates. However, there is a possible conflict of interest. How certain are we that the rater will do a great job if the issuer is the one issuing the cheque. Other models include 'investor-pays' and 'regulator or government pay', but that has not really been tested.

Under the investor-pays model, the rater rates an instrument and keeps it with him. As and when an individual or an institutional investor asks for it, it is made available to them at a price. This is akin to the equity research report that research houses perform. In short, they produce a report in anticipation of demand. The flip side is that it would increase the cost of accessing such reports, as there would be fewer takers. Hence, the price per taker will have to be fixed high. Another drawback is that there is no guarantee that the issuer will share all relevant information. Investing by retail investors without professional help will be like investing in the dark.

So, what is the alternative? Can we create a centralized agency that will have a pool of accredited credit raters? It can then collect fees from the issuer as a percentage of the issue value and assign it to a member in the pool based on competitive bidding. This would mean the issuer pays, but he doesn't get to select the rater. This will eliminate bias in rating, and over the years, a mechanism for 'rating the rater' can emerge.

This is a good idea, but like all good ideas, it, too, has another side. If the selection were going to be based on the lowest price, the CRA would have no incentive to build a high-performing organization. The more important problem is that the public may view the rating as being government-approved. That will be catastrophic, since it would give an indication in the public mind that this is fail-proof and that the government will step in to make good the loss if there in fact is a failure.

Other Thoughts

Beyond the first idea of whether we should move out of an issuer-pays model, a second view is that ratings must be kept optional. Let the issuer decide if he at all wants a rating. Since the market may be chary of picking an unrated investment, the issuer will now look for a credible name, and the rater will do a more thorough job. In the alternative, to start with, one can make rating compulsory for entities beyond a certain size. This is like making audits optional up to a level. If someone wants an audit, they can ask for it and get it done. So will it be for credit rating.

However, beyond all this, there are possibly some fundamental problems in the way rating works. In the interest of transparency, it is best to lay them bare.

It is possible that the raters have on occasion not practised healthy scepticism and have got carried away by their Excel models. There has perhaps also been the belief that the big investors would bail out the company, in the case of IL&FS. This brings us closer to the unstated charge that the raters were, in rating IL&FS and its subsidiaries, carried away by their parentage, which had big names in Life Insurance Corp., SBI and HDFC.

The mandatory rotation of raters is another mechanism that serves to keep them on their toes. After a period of, say, five years, the rater takes a cooling period. After all, a long association between the rater and the issuer can lead to a too-close-for-comfort relationship. There are suggestions that mandatory rotation can lead weaker agencies to corner business. What would essentially happen is that because of the rotation policy, even agencies that are not great will now be in a position to get business.

This, we think, is absurd because statutory audit now has mandatory rotation.[114] The other argument against rotation is it will encourage credit

---

[114]According to Section 139(2) of the Companies Act, 2013, an individual auditor shall not be appointed or re-appointed for more than one term of five consecutive

rating agencies to have a short-term view on creditworthiness, but that seems unlikely.

Rating Shopping and Other Stories

Rating agencies work to enhance their shareholders' value. So, business and profits become important. They all compete for the same set of customers and regrettably, the engagement goes to the one who offers the lowest price and, unofficially, the highest grade. Also, while handing out the final rating, the credit rating agencies are aware of its impact on the future business opportunities. There are seven raters in India—CRISIL, CARE, ICRA, SMREA, Brickwork Rating, India Rating and Research Pvt. Ltd and Infomerics Valuation and Rating Private Limited— and companies can shop around. Even in the current engagement, if the company does not like the rating given, it can go to another rater, and the rating of the first agency, under law, cannot be disclosed.

There are other potential zones of conflict.

In India, for various reasons, large long-term investors invest essentially in high-quality instruments. They are willing to sacrifice return at the altar of risk. For the issuer, if the rating is high, he can raise money at a lower cost, and at a higher volume. Therefore, rating shopping becomes popular.

Banks, too, want higher loan ratings, so that they can set aside lesser capital. Ditto for mutual funds, which then enjoy a higher Net Assets Value (NAV) if their investments are in a better instrument.

In Conclusion

In the end, it is important for the investors to take good care of themselves. They should understand that rating is only an expression of opinion—an opinion that can go wrong. It should not be treated as some form of guarantee while making investments. A talk with an independent financial advisor will also be helpful.

years and an audit firm shall not be appointed or re-appointed for more than two terms of five consecutive years in listed companies.

Finally, the regulator must build a repository of corporate defaulters to which banks and other lenders can have access. If firms can access an individual's CIBIL score, what is the great secrecy associated with corporate borrowers?

There is a crisis of credibility. Whatever the reasons, rating agencies have often not performed up to the mark. No one has a quarrel with rating changes, but if, as in the case of IL&FS, the downgrades come late and are sharp, they become inadequate. And yet, the market has been ahead of the curve, letting share prices fall and thus reflecting the correct interest rate.

Here are a few words of advice to the raters. Do broad base your board to include non-bankers. Walk out of engagements that do not provide them with full information. Compete on quality and not on price. Increase the objectivity of rating, and occasionally have a peer review done. Do all of these for a few years, and you will move up the credibility curve.

23

RBI: THE GOD THAT SLIPPED

Senior had settled down with the day's newspaper. Junior was busy preparing for his examinations. Krishna was pacing up and down, his mind occupied by what the RBI's role in general was. He aspired to be the RBI governor one day. God knows why he harboured such an ambition.

'GGP,' he said, breaking the tranquillity of the atmosphere. 'What is the role of the RBI?'

The old man decided to get into lecture mode. 'The RBI is the country's apex bank and is responsible for regulating the country's currency and credit systems. This means it regulates the banks and is in one way the banks' cop.'

Krishna blinked multiple times, indicating he hadn't fully understood everything. He said, 'All that is fine, but who owns the RBI, and how does it get down to controlling banks?'

'Initially, the Reserve Bank was privately owned; its first governor was Sir Osborne Smith, back in the 1930s. It was established as a private bank and had two key functions: the regulation and control of all banks in India and to be the banker to the then government.

'However, since its nationalization in 1949, the Government of India wholly owns the RBI, and its roles have expanded.

'As the central bank, the RBI regulates financial transactions in India. Some of its roles include issuing banknotes, acting as the banker to government, being a custodian of the cash reserves of banks and the country's forex reserves, being lender of the last resort and the controller of credit.'

'Okay, that's a lot. You need to elaborate.'

'Sure. The RBI issues all currency notes except the one rupee note and coin, which are issued by the Ministry of Finance. However, it is responsible for the distribution of notes and coins. As a banker to the government, it collects sums of money for and makes payments on behalf of the government, besides maintaining and operating the deposit accounts of the government.

'It also holds the CRR money of banks and maintains the reserve of foreign currencies. It becomes the lender of the last resort for all banks when they are in crisis. Finally, through quantitative and qualitative methods, it controls the flow of money in the market.'

Krishna understood most of what his great grandfather was saying, but not everything. It did not matter, really. As his mom had once said when she had asked him to read a popular trade journal, 'It doesn't matter if you don't understand everything you read. Just get into the groove. Get a feel of what's being said, and one day, it will all fall in place.' He trusted her like he trusted no one else.

'Can we say that the RBI is responsible for the failure of banks?'

'Yes, and no. The RBI is responsible for laying down the rules and ensuring that these are followed. From that standpoint, it is like a cop. Some of the comparisons are difficult to make. Like some compare it with a cricket umpire. I don't like that comparison, because the umpire's job is to just announce if the batter is out or not. He is not responsible for the batter getting out. A closer comparison is that of a coach, but then, he doesn't really get down to coaching the bank. One could say the RBI plays the role of a mentor to banks.'

'Would I be right if I said the RBI exists because it has to safeguard the investments of the common man in the bank?' wondered Krishna.

'Well, you have a point there, but that's not the sole purpose.'

'Agreed. Do you think that the RBI has done a good job regulating the banks?'

'Now, that is a difficult question to answer. Again, it's both yes and no. For instance, it should be congratulated for not letting India become another inflation-laden Venezuela or another forex-crisis-ridden Asian Tigers. Also, it admirably ring-fenced India against the global meltdown of 2008. But in later events, especially regarding the monitoring of banks, history has portrayed the central bank in poor light. Several private and public sector banks, along with shadow banks—NBFCs—have been allegedly guilty of either criminal negligence or active abetment in frauds.'

Junior chipped in. 'But if you ask former governor Urjit Patel about the RBI's inability to arrest frauds, he has a lot to say in its defence. His views are all put forth in his lecture titled "Banking Regulatory Powers Should Be Ownership Neutral"[115].' Senior nodded. 'Patel places the crisis on the government's doorstep by pointing out that banks have dual regulation. In that, there is the Ministry of Finance over and above the RBI. When it comes to public sector banks, he indirectly argues that the undeclared sovereign guarantee, namely the government, should, in any case, act as a moral hazard, as the government acts as the guarantee. But when it comes to private sector banks, there is better governance because deterrence comes from the market and the regulators.

'He also said that the non-integration between CBS and SWIFT had been told to the banks several times, and if they did not do it, the fault lies with the bankers.'

Senior remarked, 'Half the trouble with stressed assets is on credit analysis and monitoring standards. Inflated projections, absence of complete security cover and diversion of money are just some of the many tricks corporates play. Government must completely let go of its hold over the banks.'

---

[115] Patel, Urjit, 'Banking Regulatory Powers Should Be Ownership Neutral', Reserve Bank of India, 14 March 2018, https://bit.ly/3NWcdTO. Accessed on 10 November 2022.

Saying so, Senior told Krishna to read up a piece that he would WhatsApp him.

CENTRAL BANK COPPED OUT,
RAJAN DIAGNOSIS AND OTHER STORIES

Quite a bit of the responsibility for the banking crises must be laid at the feet of the RBI, though it has had governors of unimpeachable calibre and integrity. For instance, the bank failed in the role of a regulator by slipping up to hold PSU banks accountable for capital adequacy, fraud control or appropriate reporting of financial statements. The position with private banks is no better, especially because the RBI does not have the few powers that it has with reference to PSU banks. It is hence important that the government provide the central bank with rights such as being able to revoke a licence, merge a bank, close a delinquent bank or penalize the board of private banks.

The RBI cannot escape sanction, given that under the Banking Regulation Act, 1949, it can or does:

- Control the lending policy of PSU banks
- Determine maximum exposure and the purpose of lending (Section 21)
- Approve the auditor and can order special audits (Section 30)
- Lay down the returns that a bank has to file (Section 31)
- Inspect banks (Section 35), and give directions (Section 35A)
- Appoint officers to attend board meetings of PSU banks and ask for changes in operational management (Section 36)
- Impose penalties on PSU banks through the courts (Section 46) or directly (Section 47A).

For ages, the RBI has let banks create schemes that led to the delayed recognition of bad loans, encouraging evergreening. It also failed at the issue of wrong selling financial products. Why, for instance should the bank be into selling mutual fund and insurance products? Ideally, insurance is not an investment but is meant to provide life cover. However, in India, they get sold as investment products. While the products per se may be regulated by SEBI or the Insurance Regulatory and Development Authority, the wrong selling occurs in banks, which are regulated by the RBI. Why should banks be allowed to focus on these products instead of creating their own? The banks have a vested interest: it's easier to earn a one-time commission than to serve a long-term product.

Failed Settlements

However, it is in the matter of settlements that the RBI has been inconsistent.

Take the LVB merger as an example. That LVB was skating on thin ice, given its appalling governance standards, was public knowledge. The RBI did well to step in. But the moot point is: why did it take that long, and when it did, why did it do the way it did? It turned out to be an unprecedented merger with a private bank on dubious terms. Nobody begrudged the protection offered to the depositors' money during the merger, but why should bondholders go unprotected? And how can someone assign zero value to shares without going through a due valuation process by a registered valuer?

The RBI's role was surprising given that it worked differently in the case of Yes Bank and IDBI. In the case of the former, the shareholders continued to hold shares and didn't suffer a wipeout. In the case of the latter, the bank was rescued without damaging anyone.

When banks were nationalized in 1969, the companies that ran the banks and their shares were left undisturbed. The government set up new companies to take over the business of those banks. The companies continued to be alive with their shares and the cash value of compensation received. This helped them choose their own way of using the money.

The two regulators—the RBI and the NHB—were overseeing the case of DHFL, while several lender banks monitored its performance.

DHFL was the first case where direct public debt investors were exposed to the IBC. Finally, a resolution was made where the public got treated at par with the banks, even though the bankers could be said to be guilty of criminal negligence. After all, they had lost 60 per cent of the assets of a housing finance company. Here, too, the deferred tax asset[116] was almost equal to the immediate payout.

The road to successful resolutions is paved with haircuts and shaves of almost 80 per cent at an overall level.

◆

In 2018, when veteran politician Murli Manohar Joshi sought Rajan's help in preparing a white paper on the causes for the expanding NPA, the former RBI governor was more than willing.[117]

Rajan highlighted over-optimism, slow growth, government foot-dragging and loss of banker interest, among the principal reasons for the exponential growth of NPAs.[118] Of course, he also added malfeasance and fraud to the list. The white paper made a clutch of recommendations.

First, improve governance of PSU banks and distance them from political powers. Strong boards should be allowed to make all decisions and must be held accountable for those decisions.

Second, improve project evaluation and monitoring to lower the risk of NPAs. Do not outsource this engagement. Put an internal team in place to track costs in real time. Monitor project input costs and compare them with comparable inputs elsewhere, so as to flag suspicious transactions. IT systems should pull overall performance records of loans recommended by individual bankers, and be used to determine their pay and promotions.

---

[116]A deferred tax liability or asset is created when there are temporary differences between book tax and actual income tax. A deferred tax asset is an advantage.
[117]'Raghuram Rajan Explains the Origins of India's NPA Crisis', *The Wire*, 12 September 2018, https://bit.ly/3u9Rh2S. Accessed on 30 November 2022.
[118]*Bankers' Weekly*, 17 January 2021, pp. 22–46.

Third, strengthen the recovery process. We need both out-of-court settlements and bankruptcy processes. This will help bankers make commercial decisions without fear of inquiry.

Fourth, the government should focus on the sources of the next crisis, not just the last one. Do not set ambitious credit targets. Often, these are achieved by going slow on due diligence, which creates the environment for future NPAs. All directed lending, particularly MUDRA loans and the Kisan Credit Card, must be examined for credit risk. Lastly, since loan waivers vitiate the credit culture, resort to it only sparingly.

Incidentally, the RBI had identified a Dirty Dozen (a list of 12 companies) in 2017 and handed it over to the government for action. These companies represented a quarter of the country's estimated $120 billion bad loan problem.

How to Resolve NPAs

Banking sucks. You raise money, and you lend it. Revenues and costs are predictable and easily measurable, while risks can only be guesstimated. How well you guesstimate decides how good your profits are.

Banking involves three risks: credit, market and operational. Credit risk arises from lending activities and market risk from investment activities. While these two are transaction-specific, operational risks affect the business as a whole. Such losses happen if a customer defaults on a loan or when an investment fails. Operational risks relates to failure in any banking system, process or people.

Top management should get serious about operational risks. Auditors must flag inefficient processes, and must stand up and talk to the management. Bank boards must have modern risk management expertise to understand and act upon such risks in banks. Credit raters should worry more about reputation than rewards.

The RBI has created a loan database, the Central Repository of Information on Large Credits (CRILC) of loans over ₹5 crore to empower banks. The idea is similar to CIBIL, a score of creditworthiness of information. In CRILC, there is no numerical score, but data sharing is a good starting point to stop entrepreneurs from playing one bank against another.

Should bank staff be investigated if a sanctioned loan goes bad? Some guidelines have been put in place as to when such investigations can be launched. The idea is to protect bankers who take bona fide decisions that backfire. Bankers felt stunted by the fear of CBI, CVC and CAG, causing a loan paralysis.

Urjit Patel, former RBI governor, says no regulator can prevent all frauds, and there is a need for stringent action against the management. This is more so if the RBI has already cautioned them of a gathering storm. He argued that there are severe shortfalls in the credit-evaluation process. And one thing that will help improve regulation is if the government lets go of its hold over the banks.[119]

We must set up term lending financial institutions to deal with development finance. For better monitoring, the government must facilitate coordination among banks, tax authorities and the MCA.[120] It is important to book high-profile defaulters expeditiously, and NCLTs must deal with cases swiftly.

---

[119]'No Banking Can Catch or Prevent All Frauds, Says Urijit Patel', *The Hindu*, 15 March 2018, https//bit.ly/3WtSxd3. Accessed on 20 December 2033.
[120]*Bankers' Weekly*, 24 January 2021, pp. 24–60.

24

KRISHNA RETURNS TO HIS NOTES

Late that night, Krishna went through his notes. He wanted to convert them into a snazzy write-up for his school magazine.

He began to continue his first draft.

Auditors

Frauds happened right in front of the auditors, board of directors, credit raters and the central bank.

Many argue that if in-house people were involved in a fraud, it would be difficult to spot the crime. This is sad because insiders alone are best suited to rob a bank!

Krishna thought for a minute, smiled, and then added an exclamation mark to his last statement because he felt really brainy. He wanted the readers to re-read that sentence! Phew.

The public expects auditors to spot frauds. But the nature and training of conventional audits don't help you smell scams.

The NFRA has punished two auditors, and that is a good start.[121] Through concepts such as rotation of auditors and joint auditors, regulators are fighting back. There must be a change in who appoints auditors and pays for them. We should have a forensic audit for at

---

[121]Ramanujam, S., 'NFRA's Orders Against Audit Partners: An Incisive Analysis', Law Street India, 5 August 2020, https://bit.ly/3VUp4cn. Accessed on 13 December 2022.

least listed companies.

Importantly, independence should not only be practised but also seen to be practised. Scepticism should become a default factor during an audit.

Board

In many cases, the board was at the same time present and absent. The shenanigans inside the company prove this. Yet, the board had men with impeccable academic and business backgrounds. In DHFL, investigative journalists, who hardly have access to a company, brought out the scandal even as auditors, bankers, credit raters and directors didn't.

The NCLAT has frozen the personal assets of independent directors. This will now make them more alert. The board represents the interest of different stakeholders, but each director must place the company's interests above everything else.

A director cannot act in isolation and can, at best, initiate a discussion. He alone cannot stop a decision, nor can he turn whistleblower, because board meetings are confidential. To win, they have to group together, but turning independent directors into policemen in the board room will be detrimental to the managers' freedom of enterprise.

Credit Raters

The trouble appears to lie in the issuer-pays model. Other models include 'investor-pays' and 'regulator or government pay,' which have not really been tested. Can we look at a centralized agency with a pool of accredited credit raters? Can ratings be kept optional?

Can we consider mandatory rotation of raters after five years. Finally, the regulator must build a repository of corporate defaulters to which banks and other lenders can have access.

RBI

The RBI, whose job is to regulate the banking industry, has also slipped. It had been unable to keep the PSU banks on a leash regarding capital adequacy, fraud control or appropriate reporting of financial statements. The position with private banks was no better. The regulator has been guilty of letting banks develop schemes that delay recognizing bad loans.

The RBI has been inconsistent while delivering judgments. In the case of LVB, it valued the shares at zero and handed over the bank almost on a platter to DBS. Yet, in the case of Yes Bank, the shareholders continued to hold shares and didn't suffer a wipeout. In DHFL, the public got treated at par with bankers who were criminally negligent and this is unfair.

25

GETTING BULLETPROOF

10 January 2037

The day after tomorrow, Junior would fly down to Harvard and Krishna to his boarding school. Despite how they reacted to each other in the presence of others, the boys loved each other. Krishna wouldn't say so, but he looked to Junior as a role model. And Junior always regarded Krishna the young kid that needed protection, though he knew that one day the little one would rise very high in society, given his precocious talent.

Senior, who, each time the boys left, would wonder if he would be around to meet them during their following holidays, wanted to squeeze every minute of his time with them. He ruminated about what had happened over the last 16 years, beginning in 2021.

Cash has gone past its sell-by date. You can now walk out of a retail mall, your trolley full of products, and you don't have to wait at a cash counter. As you exit the gate, the purchases are automatically billed, and money is withdrawn from your bank account.

Banks work on a three-layer structure. L1 banks raise money from small savers, invest them in super-safe avenues and give returns in line with gilt securities. The government regulation on this is strict. L2 banks are for development finance. Corporates keen on entering banking take this route. There is no licensing; these entities offer complete banking services. Institutions and high-net-worth individuals are the depositors. The customary laws of India govern these entities. L3 banks are regulated based on size. They don't access small savings. Beyond banking, there are shadow banks—the NBFCs. Institutions that want more choices and fewer rules take this route without accessing public money.

The best and brightest people work on early detection and effective management of NPAs. Monitoring agencies receive substantial pay and have put the fear of God in organizations. All listed companies have forensic audits once in three years.

Banks have invested in financial technology companies and blockchain have had a considerable impact. With the service moving to devices and the cloud, cracking the market across geographies has become easier. While the cloud helps speed and scale, digitization connects millions at lower costs.

Biometrics have replaced PINs. Robots have entered back offices, and bank jobs have fallen by the wayside. Large private sector banks have become prominent. Strategic fit, valuations, deposits and technological compatibility drive consolidation.

Bad banks have emerged. They buy distressed loans cheaply and squeeze the maximum value out of the available securities. Thus, a secured loan of ₹100 is taken over at, say, ₹30, and the bank sells it for ₹50 and makes a profit of ₹20. The securities have become cleaner with real estate, and all investments are tagged to an Aadhaar account.

People sidestep banks to raise money. If you have an idea in mind, people with deep pockets are willing to sponsor your vision. You don't have to hunt for them. The Internet ensures they come hunting for you. Welcome to community funding. The government crowdfunds its social projects, including building roads, schools and hospitals. So, it has become essential to build communities.

Mobile-only banks have evolved. Several technologies have sprung up. These include Artificial Intelligence (AI) and cognitive computing; drones, bots and the Internet of Things (IoT); mobile; social media; blockchain; and the cloud. The integrated employment of these technologies has led to a few dramatic initiatives:

- Transforming customer engagement through predictive analytics
- Introducing service robots to interact with customers
- Utilizing social media analytics to enhance brand monitoring
- Using facial and voice recognition, natural language processing and machine learning (ML) in banking
- Analytical tools that support real-time access and offer early warnings for NPA.

Senior stopped at his thoughts. He picked up a cup of coffee and wondered how long he would live. His mind again raced past how banking is in 2037.

You do not see any physical branches of banks. Yes, there is a corporate office, but that is not one where people go for daily banking needs. In fact, they won't go anywhere for banking— it happens wherever they are. There is no signing on paper; handwriting is a long-forgotten art. Digital currencies have made their way significantly into the trade.

Every citizen, the rich and the not-so-rich, has a smartphone. Bank accounts are opened while on the move via smartphone; the KYC information is collected from a centralized database. You can also close your account equally fast.

The utility is no longer via branches and ATMs but the phone, the Internet Protocol layer and AI. Plastic credit cards have given way to electronic credit numbers. ML and AI drive banking. There are no passwords; facial recognition and credit data are enough.

The highest-paid bankers are technologists.

The regulator is now a tech supervisor geared to correct the market in real time. Technology, and not eyeballs, is used to track money laundering. A driving licence is no longer an ID proof for KYC, as fewer people drive cars and more folks use autonomous cab services. The best identity verification capability is now with tech giants. Credit scoring is an ongoing process, with every spend being tracked.

An AI assistant is your money coach. He pencils an okay or will stop you from making the purchase. For example, you might say, 'Assistant, I want to buy a bike for my son.' And it might respond saying, 'But you have an EMI coming up.'

At the mall, based on my purchase, the AI decides if I need temporary credit and sanctions it instantaneously. Banking comes to you when and where you need it instead of asking for a facility. A cloud-based personal value store linked to a mobile wallet replaces a savings account. Intelligent business value stores with accounting and tax payment options are available. The robot is your money manager and coach. It tells you when you can buy a new home.

Data scientists, ML experts, experience designers, behavioural psychologists, etc., are some of the new jobs in banking. Banks partner with people and work under a strategic business unit model for most of their functions.

Blockchain has changed the face of banking. Banks have implemented distributed ledger technology with trade finance and cross-border transactions moving to blockchain. Fintechs coexist with banks. The latter stop treating the former as poor cousins. Banks have married fintech because, slowly, everyone takes to technology in life.

How is this affecting everyone?

The number of branches has dropped dramatically, at least by 90 per cent. Payments and purchases are all made through retina banking, where intelligent contact lenses provide augmented reality solutions. The users' eyes navigate the contact lenses.

Central banks issue digital-only currencies.

Every citizen has one number, his personal ID, which is his phone number, bank number and passport number, and will be globally granted at birth. It will mark the death of a driving licence, Aadhaar, permanent account number, etc.

◆

12 January 2037

Eighty-nine-year-old Senior cosied in his slightly reclined chair, reading the latest edition of the *Business Standard*, even as he sipped a cup of piping hot coffee. Horn-rimmed glasses sat on the bridge of his nose. He didn't look his age.

Today is the last day before the kids leave home after their holidays.

Seated on the floor in front of Senior and pulling the edge of his great grandpa's kurta is the 13-year-old, who was earlier itching to hear stories of financial crime. Giving him company is Junior, who, too, has parked himself on the floor.

'GGP,' announced Krishna. 'I now have exhaustive notes on what we discussed over the last 10 days. It has been a productive holiday season. I am converting this into a 3,500-word long-form essay for publication in my school magazine. I hope the fastidious economics professor accepts it.'

Junior chipped in. 'Get it done before he charges you for plagiarizing a Harvard sophomore's speech!'

'What? What do you mean?'

'I mean, if you don't do it fast enough, you will be found guilty of having copied the talk of the brilliant Harvard graduate, Lobin Stephen Junior.'

For a second, Krishna was speechless. And then he pounced on his cousin. 'You silly moron! You cracked the password on my iPad and copied my speech. What ethics! What Harvard! GGP, this is not good.'

Junior ducked, smiled and said. 'Yup. You have such a stupid password. By the way, GGP has made a nice note. But you see, it's not Harvard stuff.' And he winked. Krishna relaxed.

The front page of Senior's newspaper had a bold headline: 'More on the National Bank of Hindustan.' The article read, 'Larissa Iqbal, daughter of the doyen of Indian banking, Lobin Stephen Senior, will head the multifunctional committee to look into the fall of the National Bank of Hindustan. They will file the report in 21 days.'

There was a hint of a tear in Senior's eyes.

He was pulled out of his reverie by Junior, who asked, 'In your experience, GGP, whom would you regard as the top banker in the country?'

The grand old man didn't give it a second thought. 'R.K. Talwar, the legendary chairman of SBI, who died in 2002. He was the greatest banker ever. He wins by a mile when it comes to standing up to political bosses.'

'I am sure you have some anecdotes to share with us,' said Krishna.

'Well, I will stick to one. Talwar became chairman when he was 47 years old in 1969. The defining incident of Talwar's career relates to Sanjay Gandhi, the then prime minister's younger son.'

Ever keen for a story, Krishna's antenna was up.

'A cement company turned up at SBI with a restructuring proposal. The bank insisted on a change in management as a precondition for further financial support. The promoters reached out to Sanjay to get this condition waived, and the finance minister intervened, but Talwar didn't budge. When Sanjay sent word to meet him, the super-banker refused, saying he had no authority to call for him. To cut a long story short, Sanjay asked for the chairman to be sacked. The SBI Act had no dismissal provision, so the Act was amended, and Talwar was asked to go on 13 months of leave till retirement. They didn't dare to sack him.

'He left the bank at 5.30 p.m. sharp; unwept, unhonoured and unsung. They hardly make any more like him.'[122]

'GGP, one last question before we retire. There has been some talk of a mysterious aunt of mine. I have never asked you. But I thought I should know if there is a truth in it,' said Krishna.

[122]Ninan, T.N., 'T.N. Ninan: The "Talwar Amendment"', *Business Standard*, 24 January 2013, https://bit.ly/3PGX2ih. Accessed on 12 December 2022

Senior's face showed he didn't like the question.

'I saw a photograph, but Junior did not know who she was, and Larissa Ma-Ma appeared unsure. I felt that no one was willing to talk about her.'

'The person you saw had immense potential, but while in her college, she walked out of the house to marry someone she loved.' Senior put on his Ray-Ban, possibly to cover a teardrop, hesitated, and said, 'It is a 30-year-old secret that the family has never let out.'

'You are in touch with her?'

'Rarely.'

Something clicked, and Krishna said, 'Private number?'

The boys were wondering if he would give them a name.

'When you are here for your summer holidays, you will meet Saloni Mehta, my second daughter, current governor of RBI.'

He rose up to give his two great-grandsons a pat on the head.

ACKNOWLEDGEMENTS

We are grateful to:

- Dr Bibek Debroy for readily agreeing to write the foreword
- Each one of the men of wisdom and accomplishment— Dr Subramanian Swamy, Dr Amar Patnaik, Prof. Madhav Das Nalapat, B.V. Kumar, Amarjit Chopra, Tarun Gulati and Aashish Chandorkar, who penned their endorsement. We are touched by their gesture
- The newspapers and magazines in which we wrote on some of these issues and the pink papers from where we sourced some of the data and chronology of events
- V. Ranganathan, the seasoned analyst, who happily let us dive into his blog and access inputs liberally
- Supreme Kothari, advocate, for providing an independent view on certain aspects, including legal
- Yamini Chowdhury for first reaching out to us, and to Aurodeep Mukherjee and Manali Das for editing the copy

INDEX

26/11, 128

Aadhaar, 195, 197
Air Deccan, 89, 90
appropriate reporting of financial
    statements, 186, 193
Associated Cement Company
    (ACC), 67, 70

bad assets, 15, 20
bad loans, xiv, 5, 9, 26, 27, 41, 44,
    46, 47, 49, 144, 146, 147, 148,
    168, 186, 193
Bangladesh crisis, 62
Banking Regulation Act of 1949, 133
Bank of Karad, 74
Basel Norms, 54
Birla, Kumar Mangalam, 169
blockchain, xv, 195, 197
Bofors, 66, 75
Bombay High Court, 60, 76
Bose, Vivian, 60, 65
Britain, 133
Buffett, Warren, 82, 165

Calcutta Stock Exchange (CSE), 83
call money, 73
Canbank Mutual Fund scam, 82
capital adequacy, 27, 107, 166, 186,
    193
Capital to Risk Weighted Assets
    Ratio (CRAR), xiv, 44, 49, 50,
    51, 55

CASA ratio, 130
Cash Reserve Ratio (CRR), xiii, xiv,
    44, 45, 46, 47, 48, 49, 52, 53, 55,
    70, 71, 73, 184
Central Bureau of Investigation
    (CBI), 26, 75, 90, 113, 124, 125,
    126, 158, 190
Central Repository of Information
    on Large Credits (CRILC), 189
Chagla, M.C., 60
Chhabria, Manu, 88
CIBIL, 182, 189
class banking, 16
commercial paper (CP), 123
community funding, 195
Comptroller and Auditor General
    of India (CAG), 26, 190
Concurrent audit, 157
Congress, 15, 16, 28, 61, 64, 65, 66,
    150
cooperative banks, 10, 133, 145, 152
Core Banking Solutions, 134, 146,
    159
Covid-19, xiii, 3, 20, 26
credit raters, xiv, 120, 155, 156, 179,
    191, 192
credit risk, 177, 189
crony capitalism, 42, 128
crowdfunds, 195
Crowd psychology, 69

DBS Bank India Limited (DBIL),
    143, 144

Deloitte, 104, 109, 110, 125, 158, 159
Deloitte Haskins & Sells, 125
Demand liabilities, 44, 46
demonetization, 105
Desai, Morarji, 15
Digital currencies, 196
digital economy, 119
digitization, 195
dotcom, 82, 83, 84
dotcom boom, 83
due diligence, ix, 42, 88, 116, 189

e-commerce movement, 82
Ericsson, 99, 100
evergreening, 22, 103, 129, 186

fiat money, 77
financial inclusion, 9, 42
fintech, 197
First World War, 8
forensic audit, 191, 195
forex, 116, 160, 183, 185
fraud, xi, 8, 42, 72, 74, 77, 92, 93, 111, 113, 114, 117, 119, 120, 131, 134, 135, 155, 156, 158, 160, 162, 169, 186, 188, 191, 193
fraud control, 186, 193

Gadgil, D.R., 42
Gandhi, Feroze, 60, 150
Gandhi, Indira, 9, 12, 15, 55, 120
Gandhi, Rajiv, 66
Gandhi, Sanjay, 199
Germany, 133
gilt securities, 194
Giri, V.V., 12
Global Trust Bank, 41, 82, 84, 85, 132, 151
going concern, 162

Gopinath, G.R., Captain, 89
government foot-dragging, 188
Green Revolution, 8, 14

haircut, 21, 136
Haksar, P.N., 62
herd behaviour, 27
Himatsingka, P.D., 67
Housing Development and Infrastructure Limited (HDIL), 129, 134, 135, 136

Icarus paradox, 145
IISCO, 67
Indo-Pak War, 12
infrastructure financing, 105
Infrastructure Leasing & Financial Services (IL&FS), vii, 34, 98, 102, 103, 104, 105, 106, 107, 108, 109, 110, 123, 129, 151, 161, 162, 178, 180, 182
Insurance Regulatory and Development Authority, 187
issuer-pays model, 179, 180, 192
IT security, 167, 168
IT strategy, 166
IT systems, 188

Jaitley, Arun, 35
Janakiraman Committee, 74
Janata Party, 64
Jha, L.K., 16
Jhunjhunwala, Rakesh, 67
Joshi Murali, Manohar, 28, 188
Justice P. Jaganmohan Reddy, 64

K-10 stocks, 82, 83, 84
Kaldor, Nicholas, 67
Kamaraj, K., 15
Kargil War, 66

Kingfisher, 87, 88, 89, 90, 91, 92, 93, 151
Kingfisher Airlines, 89, 90, 92, 93, 151
Kisan Credit Card, 189
Kotak, Uday, 102
Krishnamachari, T.T., 60, 61, 65

Lakshmi Vilas Bank (LVB), 22, 41, 43, 142, 143, 144, 145, 146, 147, 148, 149, 151, 187, 193
Legal audit, 157
Lehman Brothers, 41, 102
lemon socialism, 13, 15
Life Insurance Corporation (LIC), 59, 60, 61, 65, 104, 106, 123, 150
liquidity crisis, 124
loan melas, 9, 42
loan paralysis, 190
loss of banker interest, 188

Madhavan, K., 75
Madhavpura Mercantile Cooperative Bank (MMCB), 84, 85
malfeasance, 188
Malhotra, Ved Prakash, 62
Mallya, Vittal, 88
Manmohan, Singh, Dr, 66, 70, 102
market risk, 107, 189
Metropolitan Cooperative Bank, 74
micro, small and medium enterprises (MSMEs), 15
Ministry of Finance, 184, 185
Modi, Narendra, 28, 102
MUDRA loans, 189
Mundhra, Haridas, 59, 150

Narayan, Jayaprakash, 15

National Company Law Appellate Tribunal (NCLAT), 126, 192
National Company Law Tribunal (NCLT), 18, 19, 126, 135
National Housing Bank (NHB), 6, 74, 75, 126, 187
Nayyar, Vineet, 102
Nehru-Gandhi family, 61
Nehru, Jawaharlal, 60, 150
nostro account, 112, 116, 159

Oaktree Capital Management, 125
operational risks, 189
Oriental Bank of Commerce, 85, 132
over-optimism, 188

Parthasarathy, Ravi, 103, 108
Patel, H.M., 60, 65
Patel, I.G., 12
Patel, Urjit, 129, 185, 190
Piramal Group, 125, 126
Pradhan Mantri Awas Yojana, 125
Prahalad, C.K., 89
Prime Minister's Office (PMO), xviii, 28, 62, 64
Priority sector lending (PSL), 14, 15
Prompt Corrective Action (PCA), 33, 143, 148
provisioning, 19, 20, 23, 24, 149
Pump-and-dump, 70
Punjab and Maharashtra Cooperative (PMC) Bank, 126, 138
Punjab National Bank (PNB), 22, 85, 111, 112, 113, 114, 115, 117, 118, 132, 151, 159, 162

Qualified institutional investors, 130

Rajan, Raghuram G., 28, 29, 188
Rao, Narasimha, 66
RBI audit, 74, 157
ready-forward transaction, 68, 70, 71, 72, 73
Reddy, N. Sanjiva, 15
Reliance Communications (RCom), 97, 98, 99, 100
Reliance Jio, 99
replacement cost theory, 67, 70
Reserve Bank of India (RBI), xi, xviii, 9, 10, 12, 16, 20, 21, 22, 23, 24, 27, 28, 33, 42, 43, 45, 46, 48, 51, 52, 53, 54, 55, 71, 73, 74, 75, 84, 85, 93, 98, 115, 118, 120, 124, 129, 131, 133, 134, 135, 136, 138, 141, 142, 143, 145, 146, 148, 149, 152, 155, 157, 159, 167, 168, 183, 184, 185, 186, 187, 188, 189, 190, 193, 200
Revenue audit, 158
rights issue, 148
risk capital, 37
round-tripping, 112, 117, 118

Satyam, 102, 161, 169
SC Lowy, 125
Securities and Exchange Board of India (SEBI), 84, 85, 102, 119, 126, 148, 151, 169, 187
shadow banks, 32, 185, 195
small and medium enterprises (SMEs), 146, 147
Smith, Adam, 13, 14
solvency crisis, 124

special purpose vehicle (SPV), 125, 138
State Bank of India (SBI), 22, 74, 75, 85, 87, 90, 93, 97, 103, 104, 111, 116, 131, 150, 151, 180, 199
Statutory audit, 158
Statutory Liquidity Ratio (SLR), xiii, 9, 44, 45, 46, 47, 48, 49, 55, 70, 71, 72, 73
Stock audit, 157, 158
Subramanian, Arvind, 30, 33, 35
subsidiary general ledger (SGL), 73
Supreme Court, 20, 76, 92, 93, 100, 108, 126, 149
SWIFT, 115, 159, 185

Talwar, R.K., 199
teeming and lading, 70, 151, 161
The Bank of Bombay, 5, 8
third party's guarantee, 5
time liabilities, 44, 46, 71
Tobin, James, 67
Tobin's Q, 67, 68
Total Revolution, 15

United Breweries Group, 88
Unity SFB, 136, 137
unlimited liability, 8
Urban Co-operative Banks (UCBs), 133, 134

whistleblowers, 130
white paper, 188
wrong selling, 186, 187

Made in the USA
Monee, IL
15 May 2026

ca2726cc-571f-4786-acc4-2c0bc2906d7cR01